How ready are you to be a 7-Figure Celebrity Expert Author?

Take our quiz and find out NOW!

Go to www.CelebrityExpertAuthorQuiz.com

HOW TO BE A
CELEBRITY
Expert Author

A 7-Figure Business Strategy
for Coaches, Speakers
and Entrepreneurs

Dr. Paul Newton & Bob Burnham

How to Be a Celebrity Expert Author
A 7-Figure Business Strategy
for Coaches, Speakers and Entrepreneurs

ISBN-13 - 978-0-9912964-8-4
ISBN-10 - 0991296486

Published by: Expert Author Publishing
http://expertauthorpublishing.com

Canadian Address:
1265 Charter Hill Drive
Coquitlam, BC V3E 1P1
Phone: (604) 941-3041
Fax: (604) 944-7993

US Address:
1300 Boblett Street
Unit A-218
Blaine, WA 98230
Phone: (866) 492-6623
Fax: (250) 493-6603

Table of Contents

Introduction

How Ready Are You to Be a 7-Figure Celebrity Expert Author?

Take the Celebrity Expert Author Quiz NOW!
Go to www.CelebrityExpertAuthorQuiz.com.

This book was written as a collaboration between Bob Burnham and Dr. Paul Newton after they met at a marketing event and noticed how many coaches, speakers and entrepreneurs struggle. They took an immediate liking to each other because they shared the philosophy of taking the path of least resistance (and most profit). Here is a small insight into where these guys come from and why they think the way they do.

Bob It was 1961. I was 8 years old. My dad was an inventor and would spend all hours in his workshop creating new and fascinating gadgets. He had been working on his dial-a-line copy holder for 2 years and was planning to revolutionize typewriter corrections which were very difficult to do at that time. It was going to be a big hit. Grand and Toy had agreed to stock it.

When he finally unveiled his creation, we were all so excited. This was our family's big break! Unfortunately, my dad knew nothing about market research. No one was interested in buying the dial-a line copy holder and it sat on the shelf gathering dust. Our family struggled and dad had to go to his rich uncle for money so we could get by.

This scenario repeated itself at least 4 times by the time I was 18. I vowed that this would never happen to me. When I became an entrepreneur, I looked for opportunities that would make money immediately, or at least within a month. By the time I was 30, I had done 30 million in sales. I am passionate about taking the struggle out of business and helping entrepreneurs find a niche with money in it.

Dr. Paul I was raised in a religious family and went to church every Sunday. By the time I was 8 years old, it was clear to me that hard work and struggle made you an honest person and earned you a spot in heaven. Unknowingly, throughout my life, I always picked the hard way because I thought it made me more worthy.

I was always justifying why I was not making as much money as I thought I should. Deep down, I did not believe it was okay to make a lot of money. When I saw others doing well, I resented them and thought they were cheating by taking the easy way out. My way was much more noble and that was the trade off.

I worked 17 hard years as a chiropractor and busted my chops to make a living. After years of self-help books, personal development courses and deep intro-spection, I finally found worthiness within myself. Life did not have to be a struggle and it was okay for things to be easy. Now, with my business skills and life lessons under my belt, I realize that nothing is ever in vain. It now brings me great joy to help others spot the fastest path to cash in their businesses.

If you're a coach, speaker or entrepreneur, you have skills, expertise and knowledge that have great value. You certainly did not set out in business to be the middle of the road expert in a certain area. However, that may be where you're finding yourself. You know you have a great message, amazing prod-ucts and specialized services that people really need, but getting the right people interested can be a challenge.

Most business owners find themselves constantly looking for customers and competing with numerous other providers. It can be frustrating, knowing that you have a superior service but having to price yourself low enough so your clients choose you over a competitor. If only there was a way to stand out and make the right people who need exactly what you do, seek you out and pay you what you're worth.

Well there is! You can be a high paid expert in your indus-try and enjoy credibility, reach and trust, by writing and pub-lishing the book that is congruent in attracting your ideal cli-ent. Bob and Dr. Paul have helped hundreds of people do this and now you can benefit from their knowledge.

Let's face it. You're an expert. You have a book inside you

and you've known it for a long time. Maybe you're waiting for the right time to start writing, maybe you have a manuscript you've been working on, or perhaps you've already written a book. Wherever you are, you want that book to make you stand out from the rest. You want to be the leading expert and even a celebrity in your field. Most of all, you want to be well paid for what you do and live a great life because of it.

Dr. Paul and Bob have combined their unique backgrounds and experience to create a system that helps experts become Celebrity Expert Authors, position themselves as leaders in their fields and virtually eliminate competition. Their struggles, successes and life experiences have made them the leading experts in this field, just as you should be in yours. This book shows you how to be a Celebrity Expert Author and consists of 5 Critical Elements that will ensure that you don't waste years of your life writing the wrong book.

The 5 Critical Elements of the Celebrity Expert Author

1. Identify a target audience that you want to serve

2. Make your services marketable to the target audience you've chosen to serve

3. Write the book that makes your target audience hungry for your services

4. Speak and network within your target audience in the places they congregate

5. Offer your specialized programs to your target audience on the back-end

If you have not already taken the Celebrity Expert Author Quiz, do it now at www.CelebrityExpertAuthorQuiz.com. You will get a baseline as to where you stand and be able to measure your progress as you work on mastering the attributes necessary for success in each of the Critical Elements.

This book is written in a format that follows the attributes of each Critical Element exactly as they are laid out in the report from your quiz. The content can be used as a quick reference for the scoring of your quiz by looking up the Critical Element and then matching the attribute to the section heading in the book.

You will also see that each Element starts with 5 Supporting Questions. Each Supporting Question has 4 Attributes. You can use these questions and attributes to develop your own Celebrity Expert Author 7-Figure Business Strategy by printing out and completing each of the 5 Critical Element Worksheets at www.CelebrityExpertAuthor.com/Worksheets. By answering the 5 Supporting Questions, and ensuring that you have addressed the 4 Attributes for each Critical Element with respect to your business, you will have what you need to position yourself as the leading expert in your field, eliminate the competition and be well paid for what you do.

We wish you great success and hope you have a lot of fun along the way!

Element 1:
Identify a Target Audience
that You Want to Serve

Now that you have made the decision to write a book, it is critical that you know who you are writing the book for. The last thing you want to do is write a book that no one wants to read. For this reason, you must select an audience that your book will serve and provide relevant insights to. When you choose who your reader will be, you have begun the process of selecting your audience. By directing your content, information and insights to the needs of the people within that audience, you are targeting your material.

The people you are writing for is your target audience. In marketing terms, a target audience is described as the specific group of people within a particular market to whom the marketing message of a product is aimed. This is incredibly important for your business so you know how to position your products and services to appeal to the people you are serving. You want to make sure that you know both your target audience and their preferences so you are confident that they will want what you have to offer.

When you write your book, the same reasoning applies. If you don't know who the person you are writing for is, what they want and what they need, they will not want to read your book. If you take the time to find out more about them and make sure that your products and services provide something they are hungry for, they will devour your book. You will stand out to them as the leading expert and they will choose you over your competition without even questioning your price.

This 1st Critical Element of the Celebrity Expert Author is established when you can effectively answer the following five questions:

1. What is your niche?

2. Who is your ideal client?

3. What are the attributes of your ideal client?

4. What are the problems that your ideal client struggles with?

5. What does your ideal client want?

Go to www.CelebrityExpertAuthor.com/Worksheets and download your Element 1 worksheet so you can begin constructing your 7-Figure Business Strategy.

What Is Your Niche?

The word niche has French origins and describes a shallow recess in a wall specifically designed for displaying or featuring an object or ornament. From a marketing standpoint, a niche is defined as a specialized but profitable corner of the market. When you identify your target audience, the people within that audience must fit into that shallow recess, so to speak, and feel that it was appropriately designed to feature their specific needs. These ideal people, or ideal clients, would feel like you had custom fit your niche just for them.

Choose a Target Audience that is a Specifically Defined Market Segment that Fits into a Narrow Niche

When considering your marketing niche, instead of a shallow recess, you want it to be a narrow one. By narrowing your niche, you basically size it just so, and only the clients who are an exact fit are able to occupy the space you have carved out. When you choose the right niche, it's a very profitable business move.

There are two ways to narrow your niche:

1. Identify and target a unique group of people that have a specific need which is underserved, that your specialized service can fulfill.

2. Provide a new, innovative and better solution that no one else provides to a problem that a group of people have been used to solving another way.

But the first thing you need to do is pick the kind of person you want to serve.

The biggest mistake most people make when they start out in business is providing a generalized service that they can offer to a variety of different people. Their rationale is that if there are more people in the market that they can serve, their odds are better of getting clients and making money. The problem with this approach is that if the service can help everyone, it does not specifically appeal to anyone. When a product or service is too general and can do too many things, people are thinking, "If it helps all kinds of people with every kind of problem, how will it be good for my particular problem?"

Dr. Paul If you ask chiropractors who they can help, many will answer, "Anyone with a spine and a pulse!" They are passionate about the service they deliver and, since it can help ALL living humans, many think that everyone is their ideal client. The problem is that a large proportion of the population either does not know what chiropractic does or do not consider themselves to have a problem a chiropractor can fix. Some don't believe in chiropractic care, and some think it is dangerous and unfounded. Some people would love to use a chiropractor but cannot pay for the services.

The ideal client for a chiropractor is the person who has a problem that they believe a chiropractor can solve, who loves chiropractic care and is willing to pay good money for the service.

If you find it counterintuitive to narrow your niche or to pick a problem that only one in 400 people has because you want to keep the odds of getting a client high, chances are you will end up struggling because you won't be able to convince anyone why you're the best and, as a result, you'll end up competing with everyone else in the market on price.

Consider the bigger picture. There are 350 million people in the States. 1/400th of that is still 875,000 people. There are probably hundreds, if not thousands, of your ideal clients in your immediate area. Even if you could reach every one of them, you can't handle all that business. Not even close!

To be a successful Celebrity Expert Author, you need to identify and target a narrow niche of ideal clients who either have a specific underserved need you can solve, or for whom you can provide a new, innovative and better solution to a need that they've been addressing in another less effective way.

Pick Your Niche Where There are Not Many Other People Providing the Service You Provide to the Clients

Choosing a niche and narrowing the criteria of who the ideal client is gives you a good start on building a profitable business as an expert. If no one else offers similar products or services to your ideal clients and you are the only option, you are laughing. At least until someone else comes along and wants a piece of the pie. When many experts are servicing the same niche, there is competition.

Make Sure There Is Money in the Niche You are Servicing

In order to determine if there is money in a potential niche you have to do some research on the kind of income your ideal client has. If they don't have much income, they're not ideal. You can also look at the options they have for solving their problems. Look up statistics on how much they spend on the solutions to their problems.

When evaluating your skillsets, you need to consider that they can apply to numerous niches. If, after doing some research, you find that there is no money in one particular niche, look for another one where people will pay big bucks to benefit from your skills. The worst thing is having your pipeline full of people who love you but can't afford your fees.

Dr. Paul I live in a government town, in the capital of Canada, and it's like everybody in this town expects to get everything from the government. Everything needs to be provided to them through benefits of their work. If not, or when their benefits run out, they won't spend their own money. So, does it make sense for me to target government workers for high-end programs that are going to show them how to grow and expand their horizons? No. They may be intrigued, but nobody's going to buy. If I targeted the department and got them to pay for my services, that's a different story.

If you are struggling, it doesn't necessarily mean that your service isn't good. In fact, it can be really great, but if you're in the wrong niche you will have problems. The good news is that just by changing that niche you could literally stop the struggle overnight.

Most people have something very valuable to offer. What it really comes down to is that the uniqueness you have as a human being and your personal life experiences are priceless when coupled with your skillsets and then presented to the right people. By marrying what you learned through your schooling and your work with the obstacles you have faced and managed to overcome in your life, you get a rare expertise that is priceless when positioned properly.

A lot of us are our ideal client in our own niche. Finding our own solution is quite often why we became an expert and why we're in that particular niche. If we were checking out a new niche, we will have to do some research but, more often than not, we already know the language that will appeal to our ideal clients. Sometimes there is a slight extrapolation of your experience projected onto an ideal client. You might have to marry some of your experiences and knowledge to another person's experience to get the right words, but you just need to almost hallucinate what it would be like to be that person, project your brain into their head and think like them.

You know what you have is going to be the solution for that problem. You simply need to show how you've been through it yourself and be really passionate about what you're doing to help others with the same problem. Passion is a critical component of you positioning yourself as a Celebrity Expert Author.

Stand Out as the Go-To Expert in Your Niche

In order to stand out as the best solution for the problem you solve, you must find a way to set yourself apart from all the other people who are targeting the same clients in the same niche.

Dr. Paul For example, chiropractors all work with the body, and the spine in particular, to relieve back and joint pain. This is how the public perceives chiropractors and the main reason why they will go see one. There are also a multitude of other options like physiotherapy, acupuncture, massage and medication that people with back pain can utilize to get relief. So how does a chiropractor narrow the niche and stand out? They could narrow the niche by choosing to be the best solution for something like runners with back and knee pain. Or, since most people think that a chiropractor will crack you and that it may be painful, they could choose to provide a unique solution to the problem like being the chiropractor who provides a gentle, no force approach to back pain relief.

When you choose a narrower niche, the difference you can make for people becomes more and more specific. You end up drilling down on who your ideal client is and you can be very detailed as to what their needs are. You begin to describe a really specific problem that only the person experiencing it can understand and the more detailed you get, the more you become the expert. When you provide a solution to a very big problem that a specific group of people has, you become their go-to expert.

Best of all, when you narrow your niche, specialize and become a go-to expert, you become high-end and people expect your fees to follow suit. You may be doing the exact same thing that your colleague down the street is doing, but because you are a specialist in a highly targeted niche, you can charge thousands of dollars instead of tens or hundreds. You don't need a lot of those clients to make a great income, whatever level you want to make.

You can gain notoriety. If you can get your information out to reach those people in your niche, get it in front of where they go, where they congregate, and where they look for solutions, then you quickly become the expert that they're seeking. And you'll have more people than you can handle, beating down the door to try to get to you.

You become their rock star, and you can do this in any niche. Even if your product or service isn't that different from any of your competitors, you no longer have competition because you are their go-to superstar!

According to the client, the best solution is the one that speaks to every single pain point they have, and provides a transformation of every desire that that ideal client would have when their problem is solved. In a lot of industries, the most popular brands aren't the best. They simply have positioned their product to an audience that is going to really celebrate and love it, because it's speaking to their needs. So they've become the go-to expert.

Who Is Your Ideal Client?

Do Research on the Demographics of Your Ideal Client

Now that you've identified your niche, you need to start looking closely at who your ideal client is within that niche. Depending on the service you offer, you want to look at some, or all, of the usual quantifiable demographics. Is your ideal client of a particular gender? Age? Ethnicity or culture? Do they speak a specific language, or languages? Do they live in a particular area? What's their income? Employment status? Level of education? Etc.

When evaluating the viability of a niche, one of the most important factors to assess is whether there is money in it. Do the people in that niche have money to spend? It is important to do research on their average income. Other indicators of wealth can include level of education, home ownership and where they live.

If you are planning to reach out through social media, do you want to choose a market that is on Twitter where the average income is $30,000; on Facebook where the average is $50,000, or on LinkedIn where the average income is $100,000? If you have a really high-end product that costs tens of thousands of dollars, don't try to market it to the kids on InstaGram flashing photos of what they ate for lunch. You might be getting a lot of hits, but nobody there is going to buy your program.

Research the Psychographic Preferences of Your Ideal Client

Delve deep into the values, attitudes, interests, beliefs, activities, behaviors and lifestyles of your ideal client.

What do they spend money on? If you're in the health industry, do they actually invest in their health? If you're a coach, do they invest in continuing education programs? There are certain people that will spend thousands of dollars on personal growth and development and others who never will. You can't presume that just because someone has money, that they'll spend it on your services. You need to know the buying habits of your target market.

Little hinges swing big doors. Choosing the right target market and getting the transformation that appeals to them is a little hinge, but if you get this dialed in properly, your business becomes so much easier. Most coaches, speakers and entrepreneurs can struggle for years and never address this.

Be Able to Easily Describe Your Ideal Client to Someone Who Wants to Refer You

If you can't describe your ideal client quickly, clearly and memorably you have a big barrier to getting great referrals.

Your contacts, clients and partners won't know who is a perfect fit for your products, programs and services, even though their own peers, friends and contacts would greatly benefit from buying or learning from you.

By identifying your niche, and researching your ideal client, you will have the key points you'll need to clearly describe who they are and the problem you solve for them. This will be gold to you when you are networking with ideal clients or with people who could refer you.

Be Sure Your Ideal Client has the Motivation and Resources to Work with You

Do the people in the niche have money? Do they care enough to spend money to solve a problem? Is the problem that you can solve one that is prevalent among all the people in that niche? If most of the people in that niche don't have that problem, then it's not going to be a good niche for you.

Is it an expensive problem? What is the cost to them of not solving the problem? How bad is their life going to be? How bad will their finances be? Will they struggle or fail in business? Can you show them the money they won't make? When you can figure out their losses if they don't find a solution to their problem, you can see how motivated they will be to pay to solve it.

A great way to get people in your target market to feel the urgency to act now is to choose a problem that is really disruptive to their lives. When you get in front of these people with a solution, they will immediately see the value you have to offer. By positioning yourself as the solution to an urgent problem that everyone in your niche has, you will be able to charge a higher fee and people will see the value in paying it. You'll make more money and you'll make it faster.

What Are Their Attributes?

Describe the Characteristics of Your Ideal Client in Detail

When describing your ideal client for your marketing purposes, you want to get very detailed. It is almost like the perfect person who loves to spend money on your products and services is standing right in front of you and you are describing them thoroughly, in meticulous detail. This person is called your avatar. You want to design your book or your program to fit this person perfectly so they say, "This is written just for me."

Look to the demographic and psychographic research you have done. You want to be able to spot this person when they are walking down the street. How old are they; are they male or female; where do they work; how much do they make; what degree do they have; where do they shop; what do they wear; how much money do they like to spend on their clothes; how do they care for themselves; what do they care about; what TV programs are they watching; what magazines are they reading; what websites are they going to; do they like technology; are they into gadgets and things; what entertains them; what makes them laugh; what makes them interested in things; what causes are they into; what ideals and beliefs are important to them? And, of course, what stresses them out, and where are they looking for all the solutions to their problems?

When you know all these things about your avatar, that's the description of the one specific person you want to speak to.

Everyone represented by your avatar will run into the same problems because "Birds of a feather flock together". By liking the same things, and being in the same places, they run into the same issues and problems because they're doing the same things, they're doing them in the same way, and they're relying on the same specific outcomes of certain events. When things are good, it's good for all of them and when things are bad, that's where you come in with your solution and make a lot of money.

Know How to Get Inside the Head of Your Ideal Client and Join the Conversation That's Going On In There

Getting to know your target audience means really getting inside their heads. You want gain an understanding of all the ways that their problem is making the life they live so hard.

Dr. Paul If I was talking with a runner who is experiencing back and knee pain, there would be a big difference in the level of attention I'd get depending on the approach I took. I can choose to only talk about their joint pain; or I can go much deeper and get into all the things they enjoy about running like the freedom, the stress relief, pushing yourself and the high. When I speak to the things they love about running and are missing because they can't do it, they know that I really understand all aspects of their pain. Speaking to the distress that they are feeling due to their loss of enjoyment and to the pleasure they are seeking from my solution creates an emotional connection that attracts the best clients.

Whatever your expert service may be, by knowing the disruptions that their problem causes in their lives, and how this affects their feelings and attitudes, you also know the cost the problem is posing on them. This in turn dictates the value of your solution. The more you can highlight the pain for them, the higher the fee you can charge for your service. By really being able to speak to the desires of your target market in the words that they use to describe what they truly want, you end up describing a transformation that is so appealing to them that they will pay anything to get it.

Know the Mindset that Motivates Your Ideal Clients

Many coaches, speakers and entrepreneurs get massive results for their clients by helping them to change their mindset. The problem is that the language they use to describe what they do is usually very positive, optimistic and addresses changes that their ideal clients don't always think they need.

Oftentimes, ideal clients are pain focused and only want a solution to their immediate problem. They don't want an expansive and transformational solution. When you describe your services from your point of view, they are unappealing to your ideal client. The secret is to describe the outcome you can provide for your client from their perspective and mindset. This allows them to say yes to working with you, and you still get to transform their lives!

Know What Scares Your Ideal Clients

When you research your ideal clients, you start to understand what thoughts, situations and experiences scare them. You gain insight into what keeps them up at night. Knowing what scares them is a valuable asset to you that will help you grab their attention and close more sales.

There's a phenomenon called softening, where people soften their problems so they can continue to tolerate them. They'll say things like, "It's not that bad", "I'm not as bad as those people", and "I'm better than I used to be". This kind of stuff lets people dwell and wallow in mediocrity for a long time without ever acknowledging the cost. As experts, it's up to us to highlight the costs of staying stuck, and show them exactly how bad their life is getting because they won't move forward or change.

Bring what they don't know or won't face to their awareness. On some level, they do know it's bad and that they're hurting themselves, but if you don't point it out and turn it into a really hard problem, they won't do anything about it. As soon as it is glaring them in the face, they won't be able to let it go, and they'll have to take you up on your solution.

You really aggravate the problem. Pour salt all over it and rub it in the wound. This brings it to a conscious level where they realize they do have to do something about it. This approach is one of the tougher things for us as experts to take, because we want to be nice and we don't want to hurt anyone's feelings. But you don't do anyone any favors by letting them stay stuck fooling themselves.

Being an expert means taking a stand for the problem that you solve and telling people that they're hurting themselves by staying where they are. It takes courage to point out the problems and tenacity to deal with some backlash.

The more we aggravate their problem and communicate the necessity of solving it, the more they're going to pay to solve it. When things aren't that bad, there is no need for a solution now. When it's mission-critical, and you can get them there in a very short time, you're well positioned to offer them a great solution. If your solution provides a desirable outcome and if the transformation it provides is exactly what that person wants, they will see you as the go-to expert.

What Are Their Problems?

Solve a Definite Problem that Disrupts Your Ideal Client's Life in a Serious Way

When writing and marketing your book, always focus on providing solutions to your ideal client's problems. Talk about the transformation they will have in their lives. Describe the pain they have in their lives because of the problem and shift to the pleasure they will experience after working with you. Describe what you do in terms of their problems and the transformation or outcome they will get. They don't care about what you do. They only want to know if you can get them out of pain.

Bob When I was in Lisa Sasevich's Mastermind, I learned something so pivotal. She told us to talk 90% about the transformation and 10% about the service delivery. Most experts, myself included, talk all about the service we provide, how much better it is than everyone else's and that's why you need to buy it. She told us to direct all our attention to how the client will feel, what they will no longer have to suffer through and what they will be enjoying. In her words, talk about the beautiful destination rather than the crappy airline that is going to get you there. When I started doing this, my sales almost tripled overnight!

The transformation is the biggest puzzle piece for getting your target market's attention. The more powerful your transformation, the higher the price people will pay for your product or service. Lisa Sasevich calls your expertise and techniques for getting results the service delivery or the airplane. She describes the outcome of your service or difference they will be enjoying in their lives as the transformation or the destination.

Solve the Problem Your Ideal Client Loses Sleep Over

When you can nail the 3:00 AM problem, you will grab your ideal client's attention. You want to find out what is going through their heads when they are lying awake worrying. If you can create a picture of the problem that causes their insomnia and describe it to them, you will have gripping marketing copy. Better still, if you can describe it in the language they use to complain about the problem to their spouse when they wake up in the morning, you will be laughing all the way to the bank.

Be an Expert in the Problem that Costs Your Ideal Client a Lot of Money to NOT Solve

One of the major factors that helps in determining the price of your products and services is the cost to the client of NOT solving their problem. You want to look beyond the immediate impact of the problem to the ripple effects it has on all aspects of their lives. Most entrepreneurs do not consider this when they price their products and services and, as a result, they miss out on an opportunity to command a much higher fee while having a significantly bigger transformational impact.

Take a relationship coach for instance. Many struggle with the fact that people get stuck on not wanting to spend much money on counselors and relationship training, but what's the cost if their relationship fails? If a relationship coach positions themselves to a market of high income earners who want to protect their assets and stay married, they suddenly become a big player in the divorce niche. How many successful business people and entrepreneurs want to take everything they own, divide it in two and then give the majority of it to a lawyer? That does not even take into consideration any of the mental anguish or pain that ripples out through the entire families. It's a very costly problem.

Focusing on problems and highlighting pain may be difficult for a lot of coaches, speakers and entrepreneurs who focus mainly on positive attitude and factors that create success. It can seem counterintuitive to focus on the negative. But you need to highlight the gap between the pleasure and the pain to get momentum. People don't feel the drive to take action if they don't have a problem.

Let's look at another example. Consider someone in the personal development industry who is trying to position themself with a book. They can literally waste years of their time and tens of thousands of dollars and still be no further ahead. The costs of not being well-positioned are enormous when you look at the compounding factor of all the money that is not earned. It does not matter if you have invested in all the best qualifications, are the best in your industry, and that you could change thousands of lives if nobody can find you.

The pain is you don't make any money. You don't get any clients, and you're stressed all the time. When you're poorly positioned you're always looking for clients. You may be doing all the right things and even have opportunities to reach a lot of people, but if you don't know your ideal client, it is very difficult to be successful. If you get in front of a hundred of the wrong people and do a compelling talk about what you do, no one will buy because it doesn't speak to their problems.

When you get in front of the right target audience and your transformation speaks to their needs and desires, you don't need a lot of people. You can be in a room of ten people and have seven or eight of them wanting to work with you because you have the solution they've been praying for. When people can see how different their lives will be, you can very easily sell thousands of dollars of product and material, even in a small group of people.

Bob One time I was speaking at an internet marketing event which had been poorly promoted. There were six other speakers and only one person showed up. Because I had mastered a compelling talk about the transformation I offered, I sold a couple thousand dollars worth of programs whereas everyone else griped about how bad the day was.

Provide High End Solutions to Ideal Clients Who Will Gladly Invest to Have the Problem Solved

To see what the cost of the problem is and whether the ideal client will spend significant money on the problem, you need to do your research. You need to know what options they have and what those options cost to solve the problem. How well do those solutions actually work and how happy are they with the outcome or the solution? Are those solutions the answer to their dreams, or are they just getting by?

Factors that will help you in setting your high end fee include: how much they're currently spending on the problem, the cost to them of not solving the problem, and how happy they are with the current available solutions. If you have a really powerful transformation, and you speak to the gap between the pain they experience and the pleasure of having the ideal outcome, they will gladly invest in your services at a high fee. They're going to be willing to pay, like, ten times or a hundred times more than the going market rate.

The value of the solution and the transformation eliminates the competition. When you compete on commodity and you compete on service, you compete on price. When you appeal to people's emotions, and you show them a really powerful future, they will spend anything to get that.

What Do They Want?

State the Outcome that Your Ideal Client Wants

The key to being the go-to solution in your niche is being able to clearly state the outcome that your clients want. The biggest problem with most business owners is that they talk too much about what they do and the merits of their products and services. If you want to increase your prices and sales, you need to think about what's in it for them. What is the solution that they want? It may not be exactly what you do and it is definitely not going to be stated in the language you would use, but it will be something that you can solve with your expertise.

When you clearly state what your ideal client wants, it has to be the outcome that they are looking for, not the outcome that you think is best for them.

Describe What Your Ideal Client Wants in the Language They Would Use

When you know your ideal client, you can make your marketing speak directly to them as though you were having a conversation. This personal approach makes your marketing so much more effective because it has emotional appeal. Even though you're marketing to a demographic or a group of people, you want to speak to the individual. People like to know that they are unique and special.

You want to enter the innermost conversation that goes on in their mind. It's so important to know the demographics and the psychographics of your ideal client. Spend time around them to understand how they experience and talk about their problems. Get so good at knowing how they think that you can talk like the voice in their head. When your marketing copy, the pages of your book, and the transformations of your programs, say exactly what these people have been thinking all along, they say, "That's exactly it. This is exactly how I feel. This is what I want, and this person is exactly what I've been looking for. It's the answer to my prayers. It's the solution that I need."

You want them wondering if you have been living with them for years without them knowing about it.

Use Emotional Words That Appeal to Your Ideal Client and Create a Sense of Urgency

People only really act in crisis. Humans move away from pain and towards pleasure. If you position your products and services from a place of positive gain, and from a place of growth, people don't see it as urgent. Urgency comes from highlighting the crisis they're headed for or the losses they'll experience if they wait too long.

The language in your marketing and sales copy will be more impactful when it is emotionally charged. If you are a very positive and attraction focused person, all you have to do is look at the flip side to see how bad things would be if they did not take your advice. What could they actually be experiencing that they want to run away from? Then offer them something compelling to move towards.

Many of these situations are problems where they don't know what they don't know. But as soon as you highlight it, they can't get it out of their head. As media consultant Joel Roberts said, there's only two kinds of problems that people have: the problem that they know about, and the problem that they don't know they have yet.

Make Your Service the Solution that Your Ideal Client Wants

It is so important to clearly state what your ideal client wants because they won't hear you or take action until you do. What you're offering must be positioned as that vital transformation they've been looking for. If it's clear and memorable, your ideal client will repeat it to another ideal client, and it will spread like wildfire through the community.

Speak the language that they use within their community. Most experts speak the language of their expertise and profession because they think that they look smart and impressive. Nobody cares how much you know or about the processes you use because that's talking about the service delivery or the airplane. All they care about is what's in it for them. They want to know what transformation they're going to get and how it solves their problems.

Focus on the transformation and communicate with the language and emotional words prevalent within that community. Learning the emotional words and the languages of a community comes from talking to them, being around their meetings and the associations and things they go to. Emotions go beyond language and thoughts, because they evoke feelings which are common to the human experience. When you know the emotional appeal your transformation has to your target audience, they will see your service as the solution that they want.

—〰—

Mastering this 1ˢᵗ Critical Element comes with a thorough understanding of the target audience that you want to serve. You cannot spend enough time here zeroing in on your niche, your ideal client, their attributes, their biggest problems and what they really want. The most successful businesses are the ones who consistently study their target market and seek out more and more specific ways to cater to their needs. Revisiting the material covered in this Element will keep your finger on the pulse of your ideal client and their evolving needs. Staying current with them will eliminate your competition as you assume the role as their go-to expert.

Use the Element 1 worksheet at www.CelebrityExpertAuthor. com/Worksheets as a guide to help you compile your research on your ideal client. The efforts you place here will serve you well as you make the services you offer marketable to your ideal client.

Element 2:
Make Your Services Marketable
to the Target Audience
You've Chosen to Serve

*I*t's one thing to know who your target audience is and another to know that they will want to use the products and services that you have. If the people that you want to serve don't want or need what you have, you will not be making any sales. Likewise, if you write a book that does not make your expertise the solution to your ideal client's biggest problems, they won't read it and you have written the wrong book.

The most critical aspect of this Element is that you understand the importance of the transformation or outcome of what your product or service provides to your ideal client. When you can align the transformation you provide with the outcome that your client craves, you have made your services marketable to your target audience. Combine this with a specialized system for delivering that outcome and you will have your competition beat, hands down.

The 2nd Critical Element of the Celebrity Expert Author is established when you can effectively answer the following five questions:

1. What are your services and expertise?

2. What is your transformation?

3. How is your transformation relevant to your ideal client?

4. What is your system for offering what you do?

5. How does your system solve your ideal clients' biggest problems?

Go to www.CelebrityExpertAuthor.com/Worksheets and download your Element 2 worksheet to continue developing your 7-Figure Business Strategy.

What Are Your Services and Expertise?

Make Your Products and/or Services Specialized, Unique and Appealing to Your Target Audience

It is important to narrow the range of what you offer if you want to become a sought after, valued expert. You may be able to provide many different services that support the needs of a variety of people, but if you want to position yourself as high-end, you must dial into your niche.

Most people tend to have a broad range of services that they think will appeal to everyone. Trying to attract a wide range of customers hurts them because they are not specifically appealing to anyone in particular. You really need to have a strong appeal to your ideal client, and make your service completely tailored and customized to that person. Your products and services must be specialized, unique and appealing to your target audience.

Position Your Products and/or Services to Solve Your Client's Biggest Problems

The problems that wake your ideal clients up at 3:00 AM are disruptive to their lives. Position your products and/or services to provide the customized solution they are looking for. When you are dealing with a targeted group of people who are looking for something specialized, they are willing to pay higher-end prices. Specialty stores always cost more than the department stores and the people who shop there want higher-end products. If you position yourself as the specialist, you will have no trouble being paid well above market value.

Make Sure There Is a Demand for What You Do in Your Target Market

To find out if there is a demand for your service in your target market find out where they are spending their money. Who is already providing services to that market? Check out your competitors to see what sort of service they're providing. Look at the statistics on what people are buying and how much money is invested each year to solve that problem. If your ideal clients are spending money on those services your niche has money in it.

Charge a Premium Fee for What You Do

You must be positioned as the best option in your niche to charge a premium fee. Being the best is a self-proclaimed title. If you say you are the best solution and stand behind it with quality service, the right people will believe you. If you don't have a great service with massive appeal to your target market they're going to walk on by. Make sure you can substantiate your claim.

What Is Your Transformation?

Ensure that Your Ideal Clients Immediately Understand What You Do and How It Will Affect Their Lives

If you want your ideal clients to understand the importance of what you do, you must speak in terms of the outcome they will get from working with you. Describe the transformations and how much better their life is going to be. Tell them exactly what they want to hear, the way they want to hear it and vividly describe the ideal picture they've been dreaming about. Then make sure that your service can provide the solution they want. If they know that you understand their problems and have the answer to what they want, they will jump at the opportunity to work with you.

Make the Value of Your Service Immediately Apparent to Your Ideal Clients

People connect immediately to value that is communicated emotionally. No amount of explaining, or technical language, is going to make your ideal client want to jump. Explanations appeal to their minds and logic, which makes them compare you to your competitors. When you fall into this trap, you end up competing on price.

An emotional discussion that appeals to their urgent problems makes them feel the pain, and want the relief of the compelling future you are describing. Use the one-liners that they use to describe the pain to their wives, husbands or best friends, like, "It's just so bad that I don't know how we're going to go on" or "I don't know how we're going to pay our bills next month" or "I don't even know who my wife is anymore." This causes a vibrational response rather than a mental or thought response. When you offer a solution after you connect emotionally, they will see your value right away.

Describe Your Services with the Transformation and Results Your Client Will Get

In the following story, notice how Dr. Paul describes making a shift from talking about the benefits of chiropractic care to transformation for the client. When you talk transformation, you don't even need to talk about what you are going to do. The client becomes so fixated on the outcome that they are ready to say yes to whatever you offer.

Dr. Paul When I started in practice as a chiropractor, I was always stressed when I had a new patient because I needed to convince them to buy into the benefits of getting regular chiropractic care. I got all the evidence from their exam and x-ray to back up my recommendations and I would speak all scientifically and officially to try to get them to sign on. It was always a struggle. Then a mentor of mine taught me how to listen to the client's needs and go for the emotional impact that their pain was having on their quality of life. Once I started doing that, new patients were a joy because I got to connect to them and find out what they really wanted. Positioning my service as the solution that was going to get them the change or outcome in quality of life that they wanted changed everything. It was no problem at all to get people to sign on, and getting to be a part of changing their lives was really rewarding.

If someone came in complaining about neck pain, I would ask them to tell me about how it felt and let them talk about it until they felt they were done. Then I'd start to probe. I wanted to know how this pain was affecting their life and I would ask about it in three main areas:

1. In their work life

2. In their relationships and/or home life

3. In their leisure and enjoyment of life

I would ask questions about how the pain was affecting each of those areas until I found the one that was being disrupted. Then I would ask what they were not doing or not enjoying in that aspect of their life due to the pain. Then I would ask what would happen if this got worse and never improved? I'd wait for them to answer. This got them to reveal the true pain.

Then I would shift to pleasure. I'd ask how they would be different if this were better tomorrow. I didn't want to know that they would be pain-free. I wanted to know how they would be different in their life. This gave me the desire and the compelling future I wanted to move them towards. I'd close by asking them if, by us working together for several months, we could move them from the pain to the pleasure, would that make them happy? When I got a yes, I would know that they understood the value of my service.

It's so important to come through that emotional door because it gets your client's mind out of the way. They often aren't in the best place to be thinking when they are in pain anyway. Describing your services from the transformation and results they will get will activate their emotions.

You must be able to handle staying in the emotion with them, because it's not an easy place to be. When you can go into their pain and stay with them until it shifts to possibility of a better alternative, they know that you have taken the time to know them. It builds trust.

Know How to Increase Your Value by Speaking About the Transformation Rather than Services

The biggest challenge for most experts is that they don't really understand the outcome their service has in their client's lives. They never delve deep enough to find out exactly how much the client's life is transformed beyond the immediate impact of their services and expertise. Often, the outcome that their client got is because of the expert's unique approach and their special way of being with people. Your uniqueness is the thing that sets you apart. What's unique about you and how you are with people makes the experience different from everybody else's.

Highlighting your unique value in the service you provide increases the value at least ten-fold and virtually eliminates competition.

Dr. Paul I learned to really listen to the client's needs and go for the emotional impact that their pain was having on their quality of life. Because of that, I built a very successful practice quickly with fewer new patients who came in more often and stayed longer. The average number of visits that a patient makes to a chiropractor in the province of Ontario is between 7 to 10 visits. I know how to get somebody to come in 80 times over the course of a year. That's at least 8 times the average. And, trust me, it's no easy task for them to fit that into their schedule.

Best of all, that emotional connection goes beyond the initial purchase. Not only will the client buy more, but they will have more successes and be happier. The transformations you will see will astound you. If they believe that you're going to get the outcome, and they have a powerful emotional belief in you, your products and services will impact their lives that much more because of their belief. You will be able to charge higher prices and they will receive a deeper transformation. It's win-win!

How Is Your Transformation Relevant to Your Ideal Client?

Transform the Lives of Your Ideal Clients by Getting Them Exactly What They are Looking For

Many clients are dissatisfied when we get to them because they've tried a lot of other options, with little success. They haven't addressed the whole problem and, many times, they don't even know what the whole problem is. As an expert, don't be afraid to dig in and find out the magnitude of the problem and the contributing factors that they don't even know about. By taking the time to understand the scope of their problem, you'll build confidence and be able to offer them a solution that they have never been offered. Give them exactly what they are looking for and use your expertise to deliver it. Because you understand who your client is and what they want, it will be life transforming.

Be Sure to Deliver the Transformation that Your Ideal Clients Know They Want

Ideal clients want a specific outcome even if they are not clearly stating what it is. Most experts are so into what they do, that they only talk about their service and expertise. They can't hear the transformation that the client is asking for and never assure them that they will provide this outcome with their service. You want to make sure that they know what that transformation is. It has to be clear in how you talk about your services.

Be laser focused on what they're suffering from and what they want. Make it all about them instead of all about you. Promise them the solution that they want, not the one you think they need. When you speak that way, you will appeal to the part of them that has unconsciously been craving what you think they need. After they say yes, you will have plenty of time to bring them up to speed on what it will take to get the transformation they want. Do it any other way and you will be competing with everyone else on price.

Provide the Service Your Ideal Clients are Willing to Spend Top Dollar For

By focusing on "what is in it for them" and communicating the value of your transformation to them, clients become willing to spend top-dollar with you. Being able to feel their pain, knowing how to have a conversation about it and sitting with them in the worst of it makes you their trusted source. When you show them what the pleasure looks like on the other side, then they think that you're the best thing since sliced bread. Nobody else goes there with them.

Have a Clear, Concise Way to State How Your Transformation Solves Your Ideal Clients' Biggest Problem

Get good at zeroing in on your clients' pain. You want to be good at having conversations with them about what hurts. Be able to lead them there through your questioning and understanding. Do this gently and they will reveal their biggest problems to you without becoming defensive or trying to justify their situation. If you can go into the pain with them and hold them in it for a while, they will be eager to listen to any solution you offer them.

Communicate your transformation as the desired outcome to the pain they have just revealed to you. You'll know when your words land because they'll be telling you that you have exactly what they want. When you can clearly and concisely say this in a single sentence, you have created a transformation statement. You can download a worksheet on how to make a transformation statement by going to www.CelebrityExpertAuthor.com/Worksheets.

What Is Your System for Offering What You Do?

Clearly Outline Your Steps for Producing Specific Results with Your Clients

A system is the thing that differentiates the really good experts that have a lot of clients from the experts that know that they're good but aren't being utilized to their full potential. Experts with a thriving business or practice, who make a lot of money, always have a system that they can explain to a client before the client starts working with them. They can stand behind their transformation because they have a path that will get their clients there.

A proprietary system can eliminate the competition because they can't find it anywhere else. It makes you stand out from everybody else and you won't have to compete on skill sets, credentials and price.

People develop a lot of confidence and trust in you when they can understand how you're going to get them their results. First, you appeal to their emotions with the "what" they want and the "why." Then, you satisfy their mind's need to know "how" with your proprietary system. People love to know that there are a certain number of steps (three, five, seven etc.) and that you can measure their progress with milestones along the way.

A system also makes you own your process and your value. It makes you commit to your specialized service offering and your ideal client. With this level of certainty, not only can you clearly convey how you will help them, but you also become confident in dealing with clients who want to haggle on price.

You can easily say, "Maybe you aren't a good fit for me, because the clients that I work with expect quality and great results." You'll be able to fire problematic clients based on the standards you set with your system.

Be Able to Discuss How Clients Can Work With You by Explaining the Steps in Your System

Having your system fleshed out is only the first step. You also need to be able to clearly and succinctly describe what each step of your system will feel like to your ideal client. As you become well versed in talking in terms of transformations, you will find a transformation for each of your steps. Use the transformation worksheet at www.CelebrityExpertAuthor. com/Worksheets to create a transformation statement for each step of your system. When you can explain the outcome of each step that clearly to an ideal client, they will know that you are the right choice.

Leverage Your System and Work with Multiple Clients

Once you have systematized what you do, you can teach it. As experts get busier and gain celebrity status in their niche, their time becomes a limiting factor. Very often they start to realize that they're saying the same thing to every single client. They get smart and either record it so they can distribute it to their clients at the right time in their system, or they put a bunch of clients together and they teach it in a class format. If they're working with people remotely, they get them in on webinars or conference calls. You end up leveraging yourself, and become able to serve multiple clients in less time.

This is a more advanced skill, one that is very useful for experts who have already got their systems down by working with people one-on-one. When you are overrun with high-end clients who will pay you well for the one-on-one time, you will have the enviable problem of needing to leverage yourself. Your product suite will evolve to contain leveraged group programs as well as much higher priced one-on-one training.

Deliver Your System in an Online Training Format

Online training is a very viable way to leverage yourself as an expert. It also broadens your reach. When you can work with people online and at a distance, you can quickly take a local business both national and international. It has never been easier to work with clients at a distance. Skype, bridge lines, screen sharing and recording options make web-based programs very easy to create. Elevating your system to the online or at a distance delivery format opens possibilities for expanding your business and increasing your profits.

How Does Your System Solve Your Ideal Clients' Biggest Problems?

Make Your Products and Services the Solution Your Clients Need

Your clients must see your products and services as the solution they need rather than just another option. This is achieved by understanding what they think is best for them and then reflecting that back to them when you describe how you can help. Don't get caught up in what you think they need or how much they could benefit from your products and services. You find out what they want, you give them what they want, and once you're in, then you show them what they need.

Clients will always tell you what they want, particularly if you come in through the emotional door, but are we really listening to them? The expert who listens is the one who comes out on top.

Describe Your Service in Terms of the Outcomes Your Clients are Looking For

Always be clear about the result that you're going to get for them. They don't really care how you're going to get them there, as much as they care about the outcome. You always make the sale based on the outcome; and you keep the sale based on how you're going to get them there.

Name Your Products for the Transformations They Provide

Naming your products and services for the transformation they provide adds a whole lot of power to the emotional appeal. You can use this advantage with your products, your system, your talk, your book, and your program. Whenever you speak to who it's for and the transformation they're going to get, the right people will know immediately that it's for them.

Talk More About What Your Clients Want Than About What You Do

Remember that when you talk about yourself, people find you boring. When you talk about them, it gets much more interesting. Engaging them about their wants and needs draws them in and creates an emotional connection. Don't talk about your expertise, what you're going to do for them, and why you're the best. Talk about what it will look like when they get what they want and make your solution the best way to get there.

—ᴡᴡ—

The key to success in business lies in this 2nd Critical Element. Your customers need to care about and want your products and services badly enough to keep you in business. By making your services marketable to the target audience you have chosen to serve, you are ensuring that there are buyers with a need for what you do.

To be the go-to expert, make sure your services are specialized and high-end. Become good at describing the transformation of the service you offer and make it relevant to the problems and desires of your ideal client. Create proprietary systems for achieving your results and tailor the systems to the specific needs and problems of your ideal client. Mastery in this Element completely sets you apart from all other competitors in the market.

Complete the Element 2 worksheet, as well as the exercise on creating a transformation statement, at www.Celebrity ExpertAuthor.com/Worksheets. Use the information gathered to create your specialized system or to further target existing systems so they speak to the specific needs of your ideal client. With the understanding from these first two Elements, you are now positioned to write the book that makes your target audience hungry for your services.

Element 3:
Write the Book
That Makes Your Target Audience
Hungry for Your Services

Whether you're thinking about writing a book, part way through your manuscript or your book has already been published, the purpose of the book must be to make you money. For a Celebrity Expert Author, the right book makes all the difference in how much they can charge for their services and the target audiences' willingness to hire them over the competition.

Many experts know they have a book inside them but most never consider how to make money and generate business with their book. The writing process is not something that needs to take very long at all and, with the right guidance and mentorship, you can produce the right book that makes your ideal client hungry to work with you. With some good help and the right writing and editing strategies, you can be making money with a book in as little as 40 days!

In this Critical Element, we will cover why most experts have the money making strategy backwards and how to get things right from the start so you don't end up with thousands of books that you can't sell. Distributing your book is not something that you should have to handle, and a successful Celebrity Expert Author gets massive reach with their book, nationally and internationally at a very low cost.

This 3rd Critical Element of the Celebrity Expert Author is established when you can effectively answer the following five questions:

1. Where are you in the book writing process?

2. Who are you writing your book for?

3. What is your money making strategy for your book?

4. What is your writing and editing strategy for your book?

5. What is your distribution strategy for your book?

Go to www.CelebrityExpertAuthor.com/Worksheets and download your Element 3 worksheet to expand your 7-Figure Business Strategy.

Where Are You in the Book Writing Process?

Get Started on Your Book Now

We're talking about writing the right book! The problem is, most experts write the wrong book. It's so important, right from the start, that you are targeted and that your services appeal to your target audience.

The biggest problem is that most people make the book all about themselves. Readers don't really care too much about whether your mom bought you a pony when you were a child. They don't want to read a memoir. They really want to know what's in it for them. If you've got your book dialed in on the transformation and the information that your ideal client is looking for, that is the right book. Anything else is just not on track, and you're going to struggle.

Most people think they have a really fascinating story, and unfortunately, with all the noise out in the marketplace, your story probably isn't that fascinating. So you really have to get focused in on that transformation that you are going to be giving your ideal client. They are coming to you with the question, "What's in it for me?" every time, and if you stay focused on what's in it for them, you're already probably 75% there. But many aspiring authors are sort of delusional, and think they're more interesting than they are.

Most of us aren't that interesting, so we have to really focus on the problem and solution: the problem that they have and how we are the solution to that problem. And when you do that, they will want your services and they will want to work with you. But you really have to target that and make it crystal clear.

That's not to say that you should not share anything of yourself. Most Celebrity Experts became an expert because they had a really big personal life transformation. They were so inspired by the process they went through that they now want to share it with others and have developed the skills, or acquired the credentials, to do so.

Your personal million-dollar story is important. Writing about what you've gone through is a key part of how you connect with readers emotionally through your story. But where most people go wrong is they make it the whole book. It's important to use your story and how you walked the path so you can establish an emotional connection, but it should then lead into and set the precedent for the rest of the book and the problem/solution that you focus on.

People will buy your book for a specific reason. They might be going through a divorce, or having financial difficulties; whatever your niche is, people are going to be buying your book for the transformation or the result that they are going to get from reading your book and working with you. They don't care about the intimate details of your million-dollar story; they don't care about your $6 of ink and paper; and they don't really care whether you think they're going to be working with you later in a teleseminar or workshop. What they truly care about is that actual transformation or that solving of their problem.

Make your book be the answer, or that thing that they think is going to fix their problem.

It's going to be an answer to their pain. And the greater the pain, the more valuable your information is. You have to really communicate that on an emotional level to make sure that they understand, because sometimes they don't even really know the pain they're in. You enter the conversation in their head through your original million-dollar story and they start identifying with you. They're not alone. You understand. Then you can really talk about what you went through, and the process you went through, and some of the strategies you did to transform yourself to who you are today. You've given them hope and, more importantly, a solution to resolve their pain.

That is what they want. They want what you've got or what your clients have gotten. You have to communicate what that transformation or result is, and not just the way it will be delivered like a workshop, a CD set or teleseminar. Focusing in on that result and transformation in the book will make your services appealing. You'll sell your services as a by-product because they really want the transformation.

If you're halfway through writing your book, and you haven't identified the transformation or the result that they're going to get from the book, it's not too late. You still have time to re-focus and re-write. You can still highlight the different elements of the process or program that you're going to take them through to get that transformation. You can go back and change it into a step-by-step strategy. It could be five elements like we're talking about in this book right now, it could be seven steps, or it could be three secrets. Whatever progressive strategy name you want to give your proprietary system that's going to transform or change their life, it must ultimately get them what they want.

It's all about them and solving that problem. That's where they're going to start connecting with you and wanting to work with you.

Get Mentoring in the Writing Process

This is such an important issue, because if you do end up writing the wrong book, believe us, we've seen hundreds and hundreds of coaches, speakers and entrepreneurs that have written books that went nowhere, and worse, cost them thousands of dollars. If you write the wrong book, you will struggle and you'll struggle for years. Mentoring with those who have a proven system saves you headaches and heartaches, and gets you where you want to go much faster.

The purpose of this book is to walk you through the elements that will make your book a success and bring in money. The 5 Critical Elements of the Celebrity Expert Author is a proven system that has helped hundreds of experts be in the 1 in 10,000 authors who make money with their book. Applying these elements in your writing process will help you create success. Mentorship accelerates any process and amplifies the results.

This is the key transformation of following our Celebrity Expert Author process for writing a book. We talk about it, and guide you through our proven process, in our 5 Elements outlined here in this book:

1. Identify a target audience that you want to serve

2. Make your services marketable to the target audience you've chosen to serve

3. Write the book that makes your target audience hungry for your services

4. Speak and network within your target audience in the places they congregate

5. Offer your specialized programs to your target audience on the back-end

When you have gone through a similar process in your particular niche, and you have written the right book, your book becomes a business card on steroids that links with, and flows to, the right back-end programs and systems that generate referrals and get people involved. It's almost like a finely-tuned German sports car. You don't want to take it to the mechanic down the street or try to build or fix it yourself. You really want to address that you are writing the right book right from the beginning, because it will save you years of struggle.

Research Your Publishing and Printing Options

There are a lot of really great people out there in the publishing industry who will help you. But there are also a lot of systems that are not beneficial to every expert or author. It is very important that any package you invest in suits your needs and will be profitable. Many new authors get way oversold and lose a lot of money that they will never recuperate. If you're a new or unknown author, question someone's motives, knowledge and integrity when they tell you you're going to sell a hundred thousand books, or you're going to sell thirty thousand books, or they tell you that you need to go out and find a particular publisher.

All these things are almost myths, because the traditional publishing industry has dried up. It is so different now that people who stay on the cutting edge can do better than ever. There's more opportunity than ever. It's like the universe has come along to support Celebrity Expert Authors in achieving great success; but there's also so many people that are still teaching old principles that just, frankly, don't work.

They might work for some people that got into the industry ten or fifteen years ago and are firmly established as highly successful Celebrity Expert Authors. But even most of that old guard has really had to change and get up to speed on the new principles of publishing, writing and positioning yourself with a book. Because if you don't you're going to be left behind. It's all about making sure that you work with people who can take you through a process that ensures you write the right book that generates and attracts your ideal clients.

One of the biggest publishing myths you always hear about is the story of Mark Victor Hansen and Jack Canfield, and how they sold five hundred million of their "Chicken Soup for the Soul". He went to a hundred different publishers and none of these publishers wanted his book, but then he went to the 101st publisher and, sure enough, that publisher said, "Yes, I want your book." And now it's history; it's sold five hundred million books.

There's a very remote chance that may happen again for some lucky tenacious soul, but the truth of the matter is, it probably won't. In today's market, most traditional publishers will take a risk, but they only take calculated risks. If you have an established platform with a lot of followers they might take a risk because they know that they're going to sell a book. But for most of us, if we don't already have that platform, a traditional publisher will not be willing to take the risk on you.

For the vast majority of Celebrity Expert Authors, the best publishing route is self-publishing, because the traditional publishing route has literally evaporated. It just doesn't exist anymore. You have a better chance of growing a third eye and being hit by lightning in that third eye than getting a traditional publishing contract.

Bob I see so many people who come to my workshops who say, "Watch me; I'm going to get a traditional publishing contract." I've never had any of them come back to me and say, "Bob, you were wrong." But many of them came back, used the self-publishing route, and positioned themselves very well with the process that we're talking about in this book. They talk about the transformation, they use the book to attract their ideal clients and then they sell their services on the back-end.

Choosing a publishing route is only the first step. Part of your publishing decision also has to include the actual printing of your published book. One of the biggest problems we see all the time is people getting oversold by publishers.

Bob I was just recently talking to a lady who had been convinced by a self-publishing company to print three thousand books, because it was the only way with her colored book to get it down to $5 a copy. So she was going to print three thousand books at $5 each. That was going to cost her $15,000. And I said, "Please, please, don't do that. We can print one or two books for you, and let's see what happens. If, all of a sudden, it takes off and it starts selling in bookstores, we'll print a whole bunch of books for you right away."

In another case, a particular self-publisher I talked to in the U.S. told me that he had an author who just bought thirty thousand books. I said, "Thirty thousand? He honestly thinks he's going to sell that?" He goes, "Yup." And I said, "And he's paying for storage for those thirty thousand books?" And he goes, "Yup."

Too many times, we've seen publishers tell aspiring authors to make a big run of books, and then the boxes of books end up languishing in their basement, garage or in storage. It's just absolutely unnecessary to stock thousands of books in your home, or pay to have them stored somewhere. Those poor authors think they are going to sell them all, but most don't even sell 99 copies.

A much more efficient and cost-effective option is to work with a publisher or distributor who offers print-on-demand.

This way you can print as few as one book at a time, literally "on demand". It's a little bit more costly per book but not that much more. There are many advantages to print-on-demand:

- Your book is always available

- It's fast. When people order your book, the book is printed and sent out to your customer within 24 hours

- The production is completely automated, so you don't have to spend time packaging and shipping books yourself

- You're not sitting on, or paying for storage of, a large stock of books that may never sell

- Perhaps most importantly, if the title of your book isn't attracting your ideal clients even though the content of your book is good, you can easily change the cover. We usually end up doing so because we've gotten so good at getting our authors best-seller status and they want that status showcased on the cover.

But if you've got thousands of books in your basement, you end up married to that book as is. You're caught between wanting to sell what you've already invested in and wanting to make changes that will make your book more sellable.

It's just so risky, and you don't want to take that risk, because you don't have to.

Bob What I usually do for myself is order enough books for a talk. If I'm talking to a hundred people, I might order a hundred books. Or if I'm talking to two hundred people, I'll order two hundred books. But I won't stock a lot of books. Bookstores are not going to stock my book either. Amazon won't even carry it, unless they know it's going to sell. So why should you?

With print-on-demand, once you have the system in place and all your ducks in a row, you simply print what you need, when you need it. If your book suddenly takes off, by all means, get a whole bunch printed. But don't print the books if there's no demand.

These are just a few examples of the little things that can really trap you financially during the publishing stage of writing your book, if you don't know what options are available or the right process to operationalize those options. But if you know the right options and process, it's almost a slam-dunk.

If You've Published a Book, Give It Out

Any book is better than no book. But what traditionally happens for most people that do a book by themselves is they write the wrong book. They focus on themselves rather than what's in it for the client. Then they need to sell the book to make back the money they spent, so they focus on marketing the book rather than using the book for marketing. This gets really frustrating because they realize that it takes all this time and energy, they don't sell a heck of a lot of books, and they only make a couple of dollars a book. In the end they just park the book on their bookshelf, and then they never think about it again.

They could still use that book to start positioning themselves with talks and to market themselves. The problem is that it is probably the wrong book to efficiently meet the goal of finding new clients and making sales. While any book's better than no book, you really do want to write and publish the right book, because if you hand out a hundred of the right books, you will generate a lot of interest, generate a lot of clients, make a lot of money, and have a lot of successes with your clients. If you hand out the wrong book you will generate some income, but probably not nearly as much.

Who Are You Writing Your Book For?

Choose an Ideal Person that the Book Will Appeal to

You really want to figure out who you're writing the book for and that, in turn, comes from having a thorough under-standing of who your ideal client is (as outlined in Element 1).

Bob If, as an expert in self-publishing, I go to a truckers' convention and I talk to them about positioning themselves, writing and publishing their book, and becoming a Celebrity Expert as a trucker, I won't do that well. If, however, I go to a group that's full of coaches, speakers and entrepreneurs and I hand out a hundred of my books, I already know the transformation they're going to get. It's literally a no-brainer, slam-dunk that I'm going to get clients.

I know that the people that I like to give my book to are motivational speakers and coaches. Many dif-ferent types of coaches. Entrepreneurs as well. Any entrepreneur of a business that really can use the book to position themselves and set themselves apart in their particular niche to eliminate the competition.

Make sure that you are writing your book to your ideal client, speaking about your book to your ideal client, and giving your book to people that are congruent with the information in it. The right people will be attracted to your transformation and will want you to solve their problem.

Write About the Problems the Person You Are Writing For Has

The problem your clients have needs to be dialed in before you start writing. It's one of the most important things you can do to make your book a success. When your book holds information that solves their biggest problem, it will be of great value to them. For example, training their dog might not be as valuable to a client as turning their marriage around. While a feisty puppy may be annoying, if they're heading towards divorce, they know they have at least a hundred thousand dollar problem. If you have the solution, they're willing to pay money to make sure it doesn't happen.

You always want to think about the value of solving the problem and the transformation they will have in their lives once it's solved. Once you get that dialed in, your book, process and business will have clarity and relevance to your ideal client and you're going to be able to leverage yourself more.

Speak the Emotional Language of the Person You Are Writing For

Any niche that you are writing to wants you to know their language. If you're in the golf niche, make sure you sound like a golfer, because if you don't, nobody's going to listen to you. There's definitely a language that each niche speaks.

But you not only want to speak in their language, you also want to use words and phrases that connect with them on an emotional level. Almost to the point where they think you've been living with them in their house for the past five years. That type of emotional connection and passion, communicated through your book that's going to solve their problem, will really excite people. When they connect emotionally like this, they will have more success in the transformation. And, ultimately, as a coach, speaker or entrepreneur, is it not only your own success, but your client's success, that fulfills you?

Make Your Ideal Client Think Your Book Was Written Just for Them

When a book is written just for them, it's really dialed in to connect on a one-to-one personal level. If it's just a general, "here's what you do" book, they aren't going to connect emotionally with you. It's the difference between saying, "I'm really glad to see you!" versus "I'm really glad that everybody's here today." There's always that emotional connection when you're speaking one-on-one. So you really want to aim the book that you're writing to one person. Even though, you know, ultimately, you'll be talking to possibly thousands, if not more. You're speaking directly to them with their words in the language they like to hear and describing their problem and their transformation. Ultimately, they will get what you're talking about, be attracted and want to work with you.

What Is Your Money Making Strategy For Your Book?

Don't Plan to Make Much Money Off Book Sales

99.5% of all authors go for the big dream of selling a ton of books and making a ton of money from royalties. The fact of the matter is most authors don't even sell 99 copies. Now, that's pretty discouraging if you're making two dollars a book. But if you start focusing on the right numbers and if you write the right book, there's a much brighter picture. Most authors focus all their time on marketing their book rather than using their book for marketing. Once they use their book for marketing, quite often, they don't have to sell a lot of books to start generating money. The idea is to speak to the right audience and give – yes, give, don't sell – your book to everybody in that audience. When it's an ideal target audience, you can generate a lot of income from your book. In fact, you can have a lot of great successes and transformations even from smaller audiences of 25, 50 or 100 people.

Have a Solid Strategy to Market and Promote Your Book

You've got to have a strategy for using your book to leverage yourself, including the key marketing strategy of speaking to an audience (with your book) to start attracting that ideal client. The neat thing about it is that ideal clients are easy to find. But if we don't identify that ideal client, we can't find them. If we become too broad with who we can serve, it can be very expensive to promote yourself to the wrong people. But if you know where your ideal client is, we can get you there in front of the ideal client, speaking with your book, and then the struggle is gone.

You always want to know where your target audience congregates. Depending on your niche, you can usually find out where that is. Are they part of a club, organization, or Chamber of Commerce? Are they part of a mastermind? Do they listen to particular radio shows? Find out where your target audience is listening to your type of information. Go where they are already looking for solutions. If you know who they are, what they want and where they go, it doesn't take a heck of a lot to start getting out there in front of them speaking with your book.

Plan to Give Away More Books Than You Sell

One big mistake that a lot of authors make is they get stuck on selling their book to the audience that they are speaking to. They might sell the book for $10 or $15, but they don't realize the level of risk they are taking by holding out for that $10 or $15 rather than giving the book for free. They could be losing out on tens of thousands of dollars in clients that would enroll in their high-end programs. We really recommend, whether it's 20, 50, 100 or 200 people who have come to hear you give a particular talk, if they are all ideal clients, you automatically give your book away. Sometimes you can actually have the promoter of the event pay for the book, or for a percentage of the book, to give away.

Either way, it's not going to cost you a heck of a lot to give your book away, even if there are 100 people in the audience, because with the right book size and printing process, you can get it down to $1 or $2 a book. If you've got 100 people in the audience, it's only going to cost you $100-$200, but the business that you can generate is simply amazing and can bring in thousands, tens of thousands or even hundreds of thousands in revenue.

It's also possible to start doing some of your marketing as a Celebrity Author before the book is even finished. In fact, sometimes that's the kick that pushes you forward to really dig in and get it done.

Bob One of the first things that I did when I wrote "101 Reasons Why You Must Write a Book: How to Make a Six-Figure Income by Writing and Publishing Your Own Book," was to approach continuing education programs about teaching. What I did was I phoned up program administrators. I got through to the first one I called and said, "Hi! I'm Bob Burnham, author of the soon-to-be released "101 Reasons Why You Must Write a Book: How to Make a Six-Figure Income by Writing and Publishing Your Own Book," and I would like to teach a course to your students on how to write, publish, and make money with a book." At the time, the book wasn't even written. He said, "That sounds really, really interesting. Can you send us a course description?" So I said, "Absolutely." I got off the phone, I wrote the course description, sent it to them, and called them back. I said, "How's the course description look?" They said, "Fantastic." And we booked some dates for me to start teaching the course.

I then was sure to have the book finished before I started teaching the course.

You can start promoting yourself as the author of your soon-to-be released book, and we've done that with some high-profile people here in Vancouver. We did that with a news anchor person where we actually showed a thumbnail of her book at a workshop, and she introduced herself as the author of her soon-to-be released book.

Just remember, if you're thinking of marketing your book before it's written, you might end up having to write the book pretty quickly!

Make Great Money by Making Sales on the Back-End of Your Book

The money you make in writing a Celebrity Expert book comes from bringing them into your system and programs that are going to solve their problem. Depending on how big and costly the problem is and how valuable you make your transformation, you make a lot more money on the back-end. Most authors will focus on that $2 royalty but, the bottom line is, if you've got the right book and you hand it to the right person, you can make thousands of dollars with your specialized system or program.

Bob I've done this many times myself, and so have hundreds of my authors. I've handed the book to the right person and it's gotten me five, ten, and even twenty-five thousand dollars in sales.

I've been to places where my ideal clients congregated and I knew they had a particular issue that my book solved. I didn't even have to speak. Just going to where they congregate can be very powerful. One of the first things I did when I joined the Sassy Mastermind was to hand Lisa Sasevich my book. All I said was, "Here's my book Lisa." It turned into $38,500.00 of business! That's how easy it can be, and I've seen this over and over and over again.

What Is Your Writing and Editing Strategy For Your Book?

We are all experts in our field and the information is in our head but, unfortunately, a lot of us still struggle to get it onto paper. What's amazing is how quickly we can write and turn around a published book when we have the right strategies in place and when we give up needing to undertake every step of the process ourselves.

Create an Outline or Table of Contents for Your Book

One of the simplest and quickest strategies that you can ever do is have an editor or a ghostwriter interview you. There are a couple of reasons you want to be interviewed:

1. They interview you in a way that gets the book written

2. They will be able to pick up your voice so that your book will be written in your style of talking

First, you go through and put together your Table of Contents. For a 120-page book, it might be 8 or 10 chapters. Then have your ghostwriter or editor interview you on those 8 or 10 topics. You get the interview transcribed, have your editor or ghostwriter edit it to get the right flow, then feed it into the book formula and voila! It doesn't have to take a long time or a tremendous amount of effort to write a book. You can even be an author without having to do much of the writing yourself.

Consider a Ghostwriter for Your Book

Ghostwriters, editors and many different people can help you put your book together quickly, but you must make sure that you're dealing with people that know the process that we're talking about in this book. The publishing industry itself has evolved, but there are still a lot of people working in the old guard, and it does not work. Make sure the people that you get involved with are cutting-edge and have proven systems that work. If you deal with people like that, you'll have no problem publishing a book that attracts your ideal client, solves their problems and makes you money.

Dictate Your Book to Get It Written Fast

A great way to get your book done quickly is to have someone interview you and record your answers. The interviewer must be someone who has experience on going through your Table of Contents and asking the questions that pull out the really important information about the problem that you solve. You want someone who can do it in a way that will pick up your voice, so it is communicated to the people reading your book.

The editor or ghostwriter then takes a transcription of the interview and puts it into a logical sequence so that your book makes sense. You want to have a flow that leads the reader from the problem to the solution to some sort of call-to-action. At the end of it, it must be obvious that you are the person who can really help them solve their problems.

A ghostwriter is a lot more expensive way to do it, but a good ghostwriter that knows this system can really put together the book for you with very little effort on your part. They literally write the book 90% themselves. They might only interview you for less than an hour, but they have the information and experience to be able to put that book together for you. But once again, you want to make sure you've got the right ghostwriter.

There are a lot of different technologies that we can use for recording ourselves during the interview process. It can be done over Skype, over the telephone, using a regular recording device or even on an iPhone. You just hit record and start the interview. The neat thing is, now you can put it into a file and then send that file to be transcribed. A good transcriber can put it into a Word document that the editor can take and massage into your formatted book. It's a pretty straightforward process.

It can be done very quickly depending on how much time you have and your budget. It also depends on how much of the work you're doing yourself and how much you're getting the professionals you're working with to do. On average, if you're on the fast track, have a little bit bigger budget to invest on professional help and you're dealing with the right people, you can easily get your book written in thirty to forty days. If you're doing a lot of the work yourself, then obviously it will take longer.

Set a Date for the Completion of Your Book

Consider the analogy of Canada's Tim Horton's fast food restaurant franchise, known for its donuts. A lot of people will build their own unique one-off restaurant that takes up to five, six or even seven months to be open and ready to serve customers. With Tim Horton's, they've got this system where, literally, from the time they break ground to the time that the first client comes in and buys a donut, it's only thirty days to become operational. We're sure they pay big bucks to have their franchise restaurant built within a month but, in actuality, it saves them money. Here's why: They've got five more months of sales than the other person.

It's very much the same for writing and publishing books. You can do it yourself, jump a lot of hurdles and save money, but you'll lose those savings in time. If you do it with a professional, you'll pay a little bit more in the beginning, but it's done in thirty or forty days. That gives you a five to six month head start marketing yourself and making money selling your programs. And usually, if not always, you end up way ahead of the game because at the end of the six months you have more money in your business.

What Is Your Distribution Strategy For Your Book?

Combine Your Publisher, Printer and Distributor into One

For Celebrity Expert Author's, the publishing and distribution of their book often go together. In today's self-publishing arena, your publisher, printer and distributor are often almost one and the same. There are different channels that you can go through. For example, Amazon will publish your book for you now through CreateSpace, but we caution you in taking this route as you don't necessarily want to advertise the fact that you're self-published. A lot of people still think you're not a real player if you self-publish. But what you can do is you can private label your book.

Bob   I created and use my private label "Expert Author Publishing", but my books are actually published through CreateSpace. Buyers and readers don't know that as my books are branded and marketed using my private label.

Your publishing will be part and parcel of the distributor. Amazon is responsible for almost 50% of the e-commerce on the internet and it's growing all the time. To be a visible and successful Celebrity Expert Author, you simply must be there. Another distribution system you can use is Ingram's, one of the biggest book distributors on the planet, but you must be a publisher. However, if you line yourself up with the right publisher or self-publisher, there's an easy way to get in with them through the back door.

Have a Global Distribution Strategy for Your Book

Distribution is another area where people, particularly those who go solo or who hire the wrong publisher, often miss the boat. They don't have proper distribution. What we mean by proper distribution is people can find your book anywhere.

As a Celebrity Expert Author, when you release your book, the first thing you want is for your book to be available through almost every online and offline bookstore in the world; at least in North America, Europe, India and Australia. You want your book to be found in their computer systems. This doesn't mean that these distributors are going to stock the book; but you want to make sure that if somebody's heard of you, they're going to be able to go online and find your book almost anywhere, and that you have the means to get it produced when orders are made.

A lot of people don't find a good distribution system, and that's a problem because the people who are looking for you can't find you. You did all that work to write the book and market yourself but you've shot yourself in the foot being poorly distributed.

Another big mistake that many authors make is they take on the distribution themselves. They ship the books out of their home. We touched on this earlier and we've seen it over and over again. Yes, by cutting out an established distributor, authors can make, let's say, $4.50 instead of a $2.00 book royalty. But consider this: If they have the time to do the shipping, they're obviously not making a lot of money. That's a great indication that you probably don't want to deal with that particular person.

These are just some of the pitfalls that you want to avoid when you position yourself as a Celebrity Expert Author in your niche. Make sure the distribution is good, that your product description is good and that you're represented properly in both online and offline bookstores.

Automate the Distribution of Your Book

With the right self-publisher, one that sets you up with print-on-demand production, distribution is a totally automated system. You get a report at the end of the month with how many books were sold and a check for royalties on your book. You don't have to worry about shipping out your books, nor should you be. When someone goes to Amazon, Barnes & Noble or Chapters up here in Canada, whether they go into a store or online, they order your book and, within 24 hours, that book is printed through the self-publishing network and sent out to the customer. All you have to worry about is reading a report at the end of the month.

Plan for the Cost of Giving Your Book Away

You've probably gathered by now that a Celebrity Expert Author makes more money when they give away their books. That being said, we want to keep the cost down so it is a very cost effective business strategy.

Bob I have literally hundreds of stories of authors I've worked with, who spoke to a hundred-person audience, gave their book away, and within a couple of days, made fifteen, twenty-five or even thirty thousand dollars through the back-end. That's where the money is made with a book. Quite often the promoter of the talk will even pay for half, if not all, the books to give away. But even if you end up paying everything yourself, that's fine too.

Giving your book away is probably — not even probably — it's just the best money you will ever spend!

Here is a very interesting fact that has been documented. People who get your book and become customers, when compared to clients that come from internet marketing, in general spend three times as much with you, stay three times longer with you, and refer you ten times more often. It really makes giving your book away a no brainer!

There is a sweet spot for the specs of your book that maximize your marketing investment. There is an ideal length, size and weight of the perfect Celebrity Expert Author book. We always recommend approximately 100 to 150 pages, 120 is ideal, and that the book dimensions be 5.5 by 8.5 inches. Reasons for this recommendation include:

1. Cost: With a book that size, we can get the cost of the book printing down to between $1 and $2 a book. With such a low cost, you will have no problem giving them away. If you've got a hundred people in the audience we're only ever talking a $100 to $200 to give a free book to everyone attending. Compare this marketing cost to paying for an ad in the paper, or any other general marketing promotion. They always cost way, way more than that, and have lower return rates than giving your book to an audience full of ideal clients.

2. Weight: Fewer pages make it lighter so you're not lugging a box of heavy books around. When you travel to speak or network, the difference between a 400-page book and a 120-page book is significant. How much weight do you want to lug around, especially if you are flying somewhere to speak to, or network with, 200 people?

3. Credibility: The dimensions of 5.5 by 8.5 inches is an industry standard and people automatically accept you as a legitimate published author.

4. Reader-Friendly: You want your book to feel substantive but not overwhelming to your ideal clients. Most people aren't going to read a 300 or 400-page book. We're a fast-read society so if you can't get your point out in less pages, they won't read it. You also want the book to be portable and easy to take home with them. It needs to be light enough and small enough to fit into their bag, purse or briefcase or you risk them quietly leaving it under their chair. If they don't take it home with them, or it's so long they never open it to read, they'll never get excited about your services or follow through on your call-to-action.

Keeping your book shorter is the way to go if you want to maximize your return using the Celebrity Expert Author method.

—⚋—

Getting a handle on the contents of this 3rd Critical Element will save you from writing the wrong book. With the proper guidance and assistance, the book writing process can be quick and easy. Keep the content of the first two Elements in mind and look to your worksheets to ensure that you have effectively identified your ideal client and made your services relevant to their needs. Use their emotional language in your copy and you will be well on the road to making money with your book.

The money making strategy outlined in this Element will make you more successful than 99.9% of all authors out there. Couple this with a good distribution strategy and you will be able to keep your costs down by only printing books as needed. After all, the last thing you want to do is store thou-sands of books at your home. Use your Element 3 worksheet at www.CelebrityExpertAuthor.com/Worksheets   as a guide to create your book writing, publishing and distributing strategy.

Once you are positioned with your book, it is time to get out there and speak and network with your target audience in the places they congregate.

Element 4:
Speak and Network
Within Your Target Audience
in the Places They Congregate

O nce you have your book written, it's time to get out and start making money with it. Your book has positioned you as the go-to expert and all you need to do now is seek out the places where your ideal clients hang out. Identifying your target audience, their wants and needs was already done in Element 1 before you started writing the book, so it is not hard to start generating interest and business prior to your book launch. Best of all, getting in front of your target audience will make you a rock star!

Many authors make the mistake of trying to make money off of book sales. With a good implementation strategy, Celebrity Expert Authors position themselves to make a lot of money, even if they don't sell any books. In fact, they give away more books than they sell! By using a targeted speaking strategy and having a talk that shows the ideal client that they know the solution to their biggest problem, Celebrity Expert Authors end up with high-end clients engaged in their specialized programs.

The conversion strategy that you need to turn your readers

into buyers is the focus of this 4th Critical Element of the Celebrity Expert Author. When you can effectively answer the following five questions you will have this critical element under your belt:

1. Where do your ideal clients congregate?

2. What is your pre-book launch networking strategy?

3. What is your implementation strategy for the launch of your book?

4. What is your conversion strategy for making money from your book?

5. What is your speaking strategy for promoting your message?

Go to www.CelebrityExpertAuthor.com/Worksheets and download your Element 4 worksheet to develop the speaking and networking aspect of your 7-Figure Business Strategy.

Where Do Your Ideal Clients Congregate?

This is really about knowing how to get in front of the group or groups of your ideal clients. So how do you go about doing that?

The really fantastic thing about delving deep to identify your ideal client right from the beginning of the 5 Critical Elements of a Celebrity Expert Author system is that every subsequent step gets easier: from targeting your services, to writing the right book, to finding where your ideal clients hang out. Birds of a feather flock together! Whether it's through an association, different business groups or trade shows, we can always identify where to find them. On top of it, we can identify other partners that have email lists or mailing lists for your ideal client. By working together you can easily extend your reach. Once your ideal client is identified and spelled out, it's really easy to find where they are.

Get to Know the Groups and Associations Where Your Ideal Clients Congregate

Google makes it so simple to find the groups, associations and meetings where your ideal clients congregate. Type your ideal client with the word "association" after it in the search bar and stand back! They've got lists of all the associations in North America or the world. You can then go through and narrow it down to the associations in the niche you want to target. Try Googling some of the key words and ideas from the ideal client niche definition work you've done in Element 1 of this book followed by the words "trade association". You'll be amazed at what comes up. Google is your best friend, and the better you get at Googling, the more you can start zooming in on where your ideal clients are.

Go to Meetings and Events that Your Ideal Clients Go To

Get your foot in the door by connecting with the people who can give you access to the meetings and events. You can start off with an email and if you don't get a response, then the next step is to send a book. One strategy we use is to send the head of their association our book, and then make the personal phone call. When you do that, really connect on how you can add value to their association or group. By focusing on the value you can bring to their group, really the "What's in it for them" pitch, they will be very interested in what you do. The best thing is you've already positioned yourself by sending them your book in the mail.

You can discuss the events and activities they have going on in their particular association or community. Find out if there is somewhere you can speak, like at an upcoming meeting or in a planned teleseminar. They might be willing to send out an email to their community inviting them to listen to a webinar or teleseminar that you will do just for them. Whatever it is, make sure it's going to add value to them, because it's all about the transformation that you're going to be able to provide for them. If you come at it from that angle, you literally can't go wrong. And don't forget the fact that you've really positioned yourself with the book in the first place.

You don't have to worry about seeming self-serving because that's just a mindset thing. When you get on the mindset of bringing value and transformation to their community, your business will start doing better as a by-product. In truth, it's an issue of being valued.

Bob I always talk about Oprah Winfrey as a great example. She gives free value to millions of people around the world. I always say, "She's actually underpaid. She's a billionaire but she's underpaid." She brings so much value and transforms so many lives that money is just automatically attracted to her. She's not self-serving at all. She's serving that niche.

When we are struggling financially, most likely it's because we're not giving value to a community. As soon as you get into the mindset, and you're focused on giving value to the community that you're serving, money will be an automatic by-product.

Have Regular Conversations with Your Ideal Clients

Whether you're speaking to a group or networking one-on-one, success mostly comes down to a person's own sense of personal value. The value in your service is only as good as the value you see in yourself. When you talk to a potential client who might be struggling, and you go through some of the programs that you offer, and you know that if they even take action on 10% of what you teach it will really transform their business and their lives, you know your own value. You know they'll get back their investment of time and money over and over again. It's really hard to knock you off your horse on that. When somebody says, "I'm not really interested right now" your mindset should be, "Did you not understand what I just said? I'm really almost selling money and time at a discount."

"I really believe in myself, I really give value, and I know that people feel that they are going to move forward with my company". That's the mindset you need and what every expert needs. If clients are not getting a return on their investment and they're not getting value, you have to look at that. What is the reason that you think that they're not getting value and a return on their investment? That's where a little bit of strategizing and a little bit of masterminding would probably turn things around really quickly for you.

As an expert who is trying to break the ice and gain acceptance into a group, the best approach is to identify the things that concern that particular group or association and talk about how you can solve those issues. If you can show them how you add value to their organization by helping them deal with their pain points you always get the client's attention.

Bob Take for example, realtors. Most of them probably aren't thinking of being authors.

2% or 3% of the realtor population do quite well and the rest struggle. The reason for their success is the fact that they list and sell more houses. The other 97% are struggling because they're not able to get listings and sell more houses. Their pain point, is, "How can I sell more houses? How can I get more listings?" The top 1- 3% are very good at positioning themselves in that particular industry. You see their ads on the back of buses, benches, billboards, and in big newspaper ads. They spend big money to be known as the person who can list and sell your house. So how do you compete if you're struggling and don't have a big marketing budget? What if you positioned yourself as a best-selling author with a book on how to sell your house quickly, and for more money? Suddenly, you are able to compete with those 1, 2 or 3% that are doing well in the industry. But now you're a best-selling Celebrity Expert Author and you are actually knocking the competition out of the park. If you hand 10 people your book during a listing or an appraisal, your closing rate for listings will rise substantially.

Keep Your Pipeline of Potential Clients Full

A really great way to keep a steady flow of potential clients is through speaking with your book. If you make a habit of speaking, even twice a month, you will start to generate a lot of leads. You can speak to the Chamber of Commerce, associations, mastermind groups, Meetup groups or even start your own Meetup group. When you get in front of an audience as an expert with a book that holds the solution to their biggest frustrations, you will have a conversion rate that's quite high.

When you're speaking, always give your book away free to the whole audience. This is a highly effective strategy when there is a very good call-to-action in the back of your book. Combine this with a powerful call-to-action in your talk and you've got a one-two punch that is constantly feeding your funnel. Make a habit of speaking in front of your ideal clients, several times a month.

What you'll find is that, if you set this up properly, it starts to become self-perpetuating. You will get referrals really, really quickly. But there are other things that you can do as well. Depending on the niche you're in, you can do things like Facebook ads, which can be quite successful and relatively inexpensive. You can also do Google AdWords to bring them to your website where you give them a free copy of your book. If your book has a quiz associated with it that they can fill out, you can actually get them to reveal their problems and their pains to you before you even speak to them. You can use a Facebook ad to get them to take a quiz, give them a free copy of your book and get them into a conversation about how you can help them solve their problem. You are now highlighting exactly what your ideal client's problems are, what they're struggling with, and making yourself the obvious solution.

What Is Your Pre-Book Launch Networking Strategy?

Start Your Marketing Plan Before Your Book is Even Written

Once you decide to position yourself with a book, get your book out as quickly as possible. Having said that, you don't need to wait for the book. You can always introduce yourself as the author of the soon-to-be released book. Just make sure that you have done all your target market research, positioned your services, created your outline and have a jackpot title.

You can start positioning yourself with that book before it's even out. If you go the quiz route, you can direct people to your quiz through your talks, Facebook ads and Google AdWords. You can get them opted into your list, interested in your transformation and taking your programs even before the book is done. It's a little trickier, but it is do-able. But it really is something you can only do if the wheels are already in motion to get the whole Celebrity Expert Author process in place.

Generate Business by Promoting the Concept of Your Book

Promoting the concept of your book works to generate business because, if you are writing the right book, it describes exactly what the transformation and outcome of your current services is. If you have followed the elements outlined here, you will be so well positioned to solve your ideal clients' problems that just talking to them about what you do will get you business. When you describe what your soon-to-be-released book is about, they will want a copy as soon as it's released. If you have a method of working with them and a system detailed, you can get them started before the release of the book.

Sell the Concept of Your Book Before Your Book is Complete

If you have done all the work we've detailed in this book so far, you will have much clearer and compelling language to peak a potential customer's interest. A great way to stir up interest in people is just going to events. You don't even have to join the different mastermind clubs or become part of the association. Just go to events where those people might congregate. You don't even have to speak. Just being in the audience that's full of your ideal clients can get you lots of business if you have your book concept ready to explain. Show them the elements (or steps, or secrets, or whatever word it is that you use in your proprietary system) that they need to get the transformation they want and you'll get business rolling in quickly.

So it is possible to start selling your concept even before your book is finished. But have a publishing date in mind and a strategy in place to meet that deadline. It's not that huge a hurdle to get your book done, and we recommend that you don't put it off for any length of time because it's a key part of your positioning strategy as a go-to expert.

Consider the usual networking strategy of coaches, speakers and entrepreneurs who don't have a book they can share. Either they give people a business card or perhaps they have a brochure or handout. When you simply hand people a business card and mention an idea, most of the time when they get home from an event or talk, the business cards go in a box and that's the end of it. If people take your brochure, what they're really saying is, "I like what you're talking about, but I'm not interested right now." They're not saying this verbally but that's what's going through their head. This way they don't have to tell you, "No", and when they get home the brochure goes in the round filing cabinet under the desk.

When you can give ideal clients a book, neither of these scenarios happens. They perceive you differently. Brochures go in the garbage, business cards get lost in the box, but a book is never, ever thrown away. It will always be around that client, or it may get shared with other people. Your book might stay on the client's desk for three years. They might not ever read the book. As a matter of fact, 80% of people won't read past page 18, but they'll still hire you for your expertise, because they know that you're the leading expert.

Boost Your Credibility by Making Your Book a Best-Seller

We have a proprietary system for making your book a best-seller that has worked with so many coaches, speakers and entrepreneurs. Because of positioning and the diversity of expertise, we know that we are able to get you into a number one best-selling position in at least one category. This doesn't necessarily mean you're going to sell a lot of books, and you probably won't through an Amazon best-selling campaign. But we can get you a number one spot in your category that is congruent with your ideal clients. The only way Amazon is going to list your book is if the category is congruent, and that's how we'll set up your book. We have a system to make sure that you get to that number one spot, which really does help represent you as a number one best-selling author.

Jeff Bezos, who started Amazon, is a brilliant genius of a marketer. He knew well that he didn't want just one best-selling book out of the millions of books. He broke it down into categories so there could be best-selling books in all these categories. He knows that success breeds success, so rather than one number-one best-selling book, he has literally thousands of them in all these different categories. Our proprietary system can identify the categories where we know you'll get that number one spot.

What Is Your Implementation Strategy for the Launch of Your Book?

Build Your Marketing Plan for the Launch of Your Book

The book actually has to be published and out there before you officially launch your book. First we publish the book, get it into our distribution system and get it onto Amazon. Then we use our proprietary system to make it an Amazon best-seller, we get you to the number one spot and then we redo the cover to say "Number One Amazon Best-Selling Author".

Once the book is out, so many people get focused on having a book launch party, and on marketing the book. Our philosophy is, "Don't spend all your time marketing the book. There's only $2 or $3 per book in royalties. Use your book for marketing." So have a book launch party if you like parties, you've got some extra money, and you don't need a return on your time and investment. But if you're into making money, positioning yourself, spreading the message and helping your clients get value and transform their lives, a book launch party is unnecessary. Start focusing on getting your book into the hands of your ideal clients so you can get to work transforming their lives. And making money.

Take Weekly Action to Launch Your Book

Since you already identified some of your ideal clients and where they are before the book was even written, you should start emailing or getting on the phone and sending your book out to them. Start speaking in that community about how you can help them and give value to their community.

Whether it's through speaking to a particular association or helping an individual person, you need far fewer clients to make money this way. If your ideal client was a struggling CEO, for example, send them your book showing how you can transform their particular problem from pain to happiness. Just sending them a book with a follow-up call would be very, very powerful.

Use Your Book Launch to Generate the Business You Need to Hit Your Sales Goals

When you realize that your book is the front-end and your programs are the back-end, that's when the magic really starts happening. On the front-end, you're going to make $2 or $3 per book on royalties. On the back-end, you need to think about whether you're selling one-on-one coaching, group coaching, automated programs, or webinars. A lot of individual authors using this system sell their programs and services in the price range of $497 on the low end to $50,000 on the high end. Your $2 book that you hand out for free to an ideal client gets you leads into your programs, where the real money is. Hitting your sales goals is simply a matter of knowing how many programs you need to sell and then giving away enough books to generate your leads.

Know How Your Book Will Generate Business

Most entrepreneurial authors really think they have this amazing story and the book is just going to take off like wildfire. They believe they're going to make a ton of money and get fame and fortune from their book. This in itself is a stretch, but say it actually happened, then there's another huge stretch. Somehow, because all these people bought their book, they think people are going to start calling them up and magically saying, "I really like your book so much; I thought of a way I could send you a lot of money and get involved with you." That just does not happen! But that, unfortunately, is what is expected by entrepreneurial authors that haven't thought it through. Many authors have gotten out there with their book but they haven't thought about back-end programs, and consequently they're struggling.

Bob I had a situation not that long ago with a higher-profile woman who was engaged to a very high-profile sitcom star. She had a book written and was a very eloquent speaker. Everybody really loved her, but she was struggling. She was out there speaking but nothing was happening. I pointed out the fact that "people are attracted to you, they love the way you speak, they love your book and they want to take it a step further but they just don't know how." We immediately started focusing on programs she could offer people to take it to the next level.

When you're a Celebrity Expert Author, people do want to work with you. They want to take it to the next level, but you have to take them by the hand and let them know how you can take them there. You need to have well designed programs on the back-end that you can get them involved in to transform their lives or businesses.

You really can be a Celebrity Expert Author with a big reach and still struggle. Most of us won't sell that many books. That's just a fact. When you look at the stats of book sales, most books don't sell more than 99 copies. Even if you do sell a lot of copies there is not that much money in it. The example is always given of "guerrilla marketing" with Jay Conrad Levinson. He sold a lot of his books and actually made $35,000 in royalties. That's not a check that we would throw out, but none of us is going to retire on it. But on the back-end of that same book, through his programs, webinars, teleseminars and workshops, he made an additional $10 million on that one book alone.

What Is Your Conversion Strategy for Making Money From Your Book?

You really need a conversion strategy for making money from your book. The people in the know really do want to work with experts. The neat thing is that your book uniquely positions you to do that, and it will attract people who are more serious about moving forward. You don't get so many of the tire-kickers. People who come to you through your book are more serious about wanting to move forward and taking action. This is a great win-win situation.

Know How to Get Your Book into People's Hands

We are big proponents of "Old school is the new school." We know that many gurus out there are teaching people how to leverage the internet and social media. But we like, and have consistently achieved great success with, the good old-fashioned methods of connecting with people. Some things never get old like face-to-face meetings, public speaking and printed books. Get in front of your target audience with your book and give them away.

You could sell your book at $15 or $20 to a small number of people at a talk, but if they're all your ideal clients, you're always better off giving it away with a powerful call-to-action. Even if there's a hundred people in that audience, with a production cost of $1 to $2 per book, you're still only spending $100 to $200, which you might even be able to get covered by, or at least shared with, the event promoter or organization.

Anytime you have the opportunity to meet with qualified potential buyers for your programs, products or services – whether it's speaking at an event, meeting people at someone else's event or at a networking function, or meeting a potential client for the first time – always have books on hand to give away. We like to refer to your book as "a business card on steroids". Business cards get tossed into a box on their desk. Brochures and pamphlets go into the circular filing system under their desk. But a book will sit on their desk, or better yet, their bedside table. In time, it might be shared with someone else, but it will never, ever, be thrown away.

We don't want to ignore the fact that people will look for you online. Your online strategies and structures need to be established so that those who are looking for someone in your area of expertise can easily find you.

Not only does your book need to be published on established distributors like Amazon, but you need to be listed high up in the category that's congruent with your ideal clients. Our system sets your book up to get you to the number one spot in your category, which in turn helps represent you as a number one best-selling author.

If you have a website, you need to be ranked high on search engines like Google. Your social media should drive people to your website and/or to your listing on Amazon. Any online outreach, be it a blog, ezine or even your email signature, should promote and link to your book. Your book has the power to transform people's lives. Be proud, and shameless, in promoting it everywhere and anywhere you can.

Have a Targeted Give Away Strategy for Your Book

Many authors are worried about devaluing their book or wasting their energy by giving it to anybody and everybody. In most cases, if you really identify your ideal clients and the associations and organizations where they hang around, it's never a devaluing or waste of your book. Yes, there may be some that aren't quite your ideal client, but maybe they know someone who is. You could also give away your book to all the people who, for example, might sign up for a quiz. You give away your free book to sign up for a quiz, or you can give everybody a free book after the quiz is completed. When you get the costs of your book down so low, it simply becomes part of doing business.

Compare this with an ad in a local paper today, which can easily cost you a thousand dollars. It may be circulated to 60,000 people locally but only 100 might be your ideal client. Of those 100, how many of them will be reading that particular paper at the time your ad is run? The odds are almost zero that you'll get anything from an ad like that. But when you're speaking to an association of ideal clients, while you might be giving away books that won't always hit the target, your costs are really not worth talking about because you're getting so many people who are going to take it to the next step.

This is why it's so important to have a call-to-action in your book. You want to turn the reader into a client.

Know How to Turn a Reader of Your Book into a Client

First, you have to be extremely passionate about what you do. You wouldn't be reading this book if you weren't passionate about what you do and about writing a book to promote your services. Your passion is what's really going to attract, through your book, that person or organization to you. So passion is a big part.

The other key to turning a reader into a client is to have a compelling call-to-action, right in the book. One of our favorite things to do is a quiz, where you actually send them to a website where they take a 25 to 100-question quiz. The results are sent to you directly, so you can then call and go through the results with them in a discovery session or strategy session. You may want to have a pre-prepared action plan form to follow during your session with them. The neat thing about a quiz is that it really shows where your client is strong, but it also shows where your clients are weak. You're going to really identify the pain points, the problems that they have, and how you can solve them. Not only will you see how you can best help them, but they are going to see where they need help too. Your client is already starting to see that you are the ideal person to help them through their pain points just by doing a quiz. The fact that they will take the time to do the quiz also shows you that they are somebody who is going to take action and are somebody who is interested. You reduce the likelihood of someone who just wants to talk to you for an hour and waste your time.

Get Good at the Sales Conversation and Closing the Sale

The way to guide potential clients to being a buyer is to connect with them on an emotional level. Whatever you're helping them with, whether it's business or personal, you want to start asking questions on the biggest issues that they're dealing with. Where is it that they just can't seem to move forward? If you developed a quiz, it has already shown you where they are struggling, so now you want to have an initial discovery session and get them talking about those points that they're struggling with. Once they're talking about their biggest issues, you want to emphasize those points so that you connect with them emotionally on their struggles. If you're good at the whole idea of asking questions about how those struggles have affected them, both in business and possibly personally, they'll connect with some of the issues, and in a lot of cases, hear for the first time the reasons they are struggling.

For example, why they have anxiety or why they wake up in the middle of the night. Just by asking the questions in a discovery session, you'll be bringing light to things they hadn't really thought about.

Take notes on their description of their struggles. And shift your questioning to what it would be like to have those issues resolved. This is where your notes become extremely valuable because they're going to start telling you things like, "It would be so nice to not have to struggle about money, and to have a holiday a couple of times a year" or "It'd be so nice to start getting involved with my spouse and not fight about money." They're going to start telling you in their own words how they would like their problems to be solved. At that point of the session, you can ask them: "How do you think I can help you?" The neat thing with this question is they will go into a process of starting to list all these different ways that you can help them. They actually give you your own sales copy.

What's happened is you've identified their problems, you've aggravated them, and you've repeated them back in their own words. They have also told you exactly how they would like you to help them. At that point you don't have to sell them anything, because they will sell themselves with their own sales copy. Once they've realized what they want you to help them with, because you're already in that niche and that's what you do, you can say "Yes, I have a program for that, and this is exactly how I can help you with those issues."

You just tell them the price and wait for them to say yes. It's really important that when you state your price, they should be the next person to talk. If you state that your price is $4,500, for example, but I can give it to you at a discount of... that means you don't believe in your price. Sometimes it only takes them a quarter of a second to respond, sometimes it's thirty seconds later and they don't know what to say. But they have to respond next and what you'll get is a definite answer of yes or no.

What Is Your Speaking Strategy for Promoting Your Message?

Speak Regularly on the Solutions You Provide for Your Ideal Clients

Nothing's going to happen for any of us unless we take action. So speaking even twice a month on a regular basis will start building a really great business out of the back-end of your book. If you're an energetic person and you like to go gangbusters, you can focus on speaking and networking with different groups a couple of times a week. You'll be amazed at how fast your whole business will start growing. In fact, in a short amount of time, you won't even be able to keep up with it.

You can start locally, or you can go nationally. Whatever you prefer. Obviously, locally is going to cost a lot less as nationally involves travel and expenses. Start identifying where your ideal clients are physically. Email them or phone them and send them a copy of your book; then start going through these strategies of how you can really help their community and give great value and solve their problems. So, put it on your calendar that you're going to contact, for example, at least two people a week that are in your ideal client community, and follow through diligently every week.

Get in Front of Your Target Audience and Show Them What You Can Do

If potential clients are already trying to solve problems and you show up in their community positioned with your book, you're setting yourself apart from anyone else who's been in that community. If you've got systems and programs on the back-end of your book, you give your book away and you talk about your solutions and transformations, they will readily start working with you.

Because they are so emotionally motivated by the solution or transformation, quite often they're not even really aware whether they bought a workshop or a one-on-one with you. They don't really care whether it's a 6-CD set, a workshop, an event or whatever it is; they want the transformation. Anywhere your clients are already gathered working on these particular issues and problems, if you go with a book and position yourself, you're going to get a great welcome.

Give a Talk that Converts Your Target Audience into Clients

A talk isn't just a talk. This is another key component to the Celebrity Expert Author positioning strategy. You can be witty, you can be funny, people can like you as a speaker, but if you don't convert, you're wasting your time. Lisa Sasevich, one of our mentors, calls it a speak-to-sell strategy. We call it a speak-to-call-to-action strategy. You take them from the beginning of your talk through a strategy whereby, at the end of the talk, they sign up for a strategy session or some other sort of call-to-action. This is a deliberate approach, and there are several key steps to follow, that will radically increase your chances that the speak-to-sell or speak-to-call-to-action is actually done.

Remember an earlier reference to a woman who was giving talks and everybody loved her (in Element 4, "I Know My Book Will Generate Success")? She was selling quite a number of books but wasn't getting any traction. She was making a couple of bucks on the book sales but was not cashing in on the back-end sales. She did not have a strategy in her talk to take them from resonating with her story, to identifying a specific problem they had, to seeing her as the obvious solution, and then to taking immediate action. When you go through that process in a logical manner, you'll start converting a lot of people in an audience of ideal clients.

Get Paid Well When You Speak

Much like the publishing industry has evolved from traditional to self-publishing, the speaking industry is changing as well. North America has many speaking associations, and a lot of them still deal with fee-based speaking. However, the fee-based speaking industry is, in general, drying up. Many speakers still hold out for these $5,000 or $10,000 fees but if you speak for free, with your book, you'll get lots of people that will have you speak at their industry event.

Rather than going for the $5,000, $10,000 or $15,000 keynote speaker fee on the front-end, take them into a process where they get involved with you through a back-end process that gets them into your programs. It's not uncommon for one of our authors to do a free talk where there are 100 people in the audience and walk away with 5 or 6 figures in back-end sales.

—◊—

When it comes time to make money from your book, your speaking and networking strategy will be paramount. With well targeted clients, it is very easy to find them and get in front of them where you are well positioned. You may have found that the prior Elements of the Celebrity Expert Author already set you up to network and market your services well within your target audience. By strategically implementing even only 10% of the content we have shared with you, you will begin to make good money from your book.

The keys to success with this 4th Element are a specialized, high-end offer, an engaging talk that converts and a sales conversation strategy that turns leads into clients. Use the Element 4 worksheet at www.CelebrityExpertAuthor.com/Worksheets to assist you with the implementation of strategies from this Element. We also have resources on our website to assist you with creating a talk that converts and takes clients from cold to sold.

The next step is to offer your specialized programs to your target audience on the back-end.

Element 5:
Offer Your Specialized Programs
to Your Target Audience
on the Back-End

The real money in a book lies in the specialized programs that you sell to your ideal clients on the back-end. This is what makes Celebrity Expert Authors stand out from all the competition in the marketplace. They have a specialized system with clearly defined steps to achieve the transformation or outcome that their target market craves. They base their fees on their systems for producing particular transformations, rather than the number of hours they work. As a result, they can bill hundreds, even thousands, of dollars more than their competitors.

In this Critical Element, we will discuss the importance of chunking your services into specialized products so you have a way of keeping your clients engaged long term. Having a customizable product suite gives you the ability to give your clients exactly what they need at the given moment and to offer them additional help as they need it. Some of your services may involve your time one-on-one. Others can be offered as products that don't require your time, or as group programs where you can serve many people at once.

The way you structure your specialized programs and product suite will be the key to how you sell your services and how much money you can make from your book. This 5th Critical Element of the Celebrity Expert Author is established when you can effectively answer the following five questions:

1. What specialized programs do you have for delivering your outcomes?

2. How have you removed yourself from the fee for service model?

3. How do you engage your clients long term?

4. What group programs do you offer to leverage your time?

5. How does your product suite showcase your services and expertise?

Go to www.CelebrityExpertAuthor.com/Worksheets to download your Element 5 worksheet and flesh out the back-end of your 7-Figure Business Strategy.

What Specialized Programs Do You Have for Delivering Your Outcomes?

Create Your Specialized Programs with Steps to Generate Specific Client Outcomes

The place where you will make the most money with this system is through the sale of your specialized programs. If you don't already have one, this is something that you're going to want to build fast. This is truly where you're going to make the money on the back-end of your book and your business. If you already have a specialized program, it is important that you have created steps within the program that generate specific client outcomes.

It is very important to instill confidence in the client. Up until now, we've been talking so much about getting them hooked by the transformation and by the emotional leverage that makes them want to engage with you. But then you do have to deliver the outcome. If you have been getting results and delivering outcomes, time and again, you have a system. The question is whether your system has been fleshed out and a series of steps clearly delineated. What will really set you apart from other people in your field is having a series of steps that get a specialized outcome. That specialized outcome is going to be of paramount importance in growing your book and your business.

Have Programs and Packages Ready to Sell

The next thing you need to cash in on in the business is programs and packages that are priced properly and ready to sell. The way you put your services together and value them is going to have a huge impact on your positioning, how you are perceived and how much money you make.

Systems and programs that are way too packed with content and information can overwhelm your client and negatively impact the results you get. A lot of people put so much content in their first program that it could, even should, be broken down into three or four more targeted marketable programs. In order to deliver true value to your client, you need to get them good results, in neat packages, in all areas of your service.

Often, you can take pieces of your system and package them and price them on their own for a lot more than you think. When they're delivered properly, they can provide enormous value and transformation for your client.

This makes it simpler for your clients, as it doesn't overwhelm them and keeps them moving forward. It also allows for the malleability and fun of putting together something customized for a client. If you take your system, pull it apart, and package and price all the parts of it, then one client could enter the system at step two, while others might come in at step one, depending on what they've already got done and what will serve them best. If you have all your packages and programs ready-made and modular, you can deliver your transformation at any starting point.

There are also many different ways to run a program. You can work with somebody one-on-one with your coaching program, or you can put people into a group class. You can teach in person or use the internet or teleseminar method.

When you've got a combination of tailor-made and automated systems, and you have a process for selling your system, this is where the magic starts.

Have a Process for Selling Your Packages and Programs

There are many selling strategies out there, and a lot of people in this industry are attracted to the teleseminar and internet sales page method of filling their programs. Our definite favorites remain the good old fashioned methods of meeting people, speaking, giving them your book and following up with a personal email or phone call. We are of the philosophy that "Old school is the new school". While there are many trends in marketing, the personal connection will never get old. But we certainly don't advocate being a dinosaur. We also get people involved through Facebook ads and Google AdWords.

Once you get positioned with this book, most selling strategies out there are so adaptable and so easily fit into various systems and sales opportunities. Continuing education programs can be an excellent source for finding your ideal clients, and they often have the dual advantage of both paying you to teach the class while also bringing you ideal clients. You can speak at, or create your own, Meetup. You'll be able to confidently go out and speak anywhere that your ideal clients congregate, like masterminds or teleseminars. Even focusing on just a couple of these systems will cause magic to happen in expanding your business.

Have a Method for Taking Payment from Clients

When you are doing business this way, you'll want to make sure you can take payment promptly. Setting up a process where you can process people's credit cards is something you have to get set up right from the beginning. The basic starter system is PayPal, which can work well to a certain point when you're just starting out. There are different low-cost methods now, like the Square, that allow you to swipe credit cards and process payments through your smartphone or tablet. If you offer payment plans, you need to set up and accept automated payments. In Canada and the U.S. there are different systems that will deposit money directly into your bank account.

If you are looking to integrate this with a website, first you'll need a merchant account and then you'll need to set up some sort of shopping cart like 1ShoppingCart or Infusionsoft.

If you're out speaking and somebody wants to buy one of your programs, we always recommend that you get their credit card processed as quickly as possible. Don't take the chance of giving them a link or URL to do it at home because, even though they have good intentions, human nature is such that by the time they get home, they usually don't do it. Always have the processing part of your sale on-site, in your immediate control, because if people don't take action, they lose out and you lose out.

The payment is a big part of the commitment of them saying "Yes." And once it's done, they are less likely to un-sell themselves.

How Have You Removed Yourself from the Fee for Service Model?

Don't Exchange Dollars for Hours

A big leap for entrepreneurs is to go from fee for service to fee for transformation. The problem that most run into when they become experts is they're not getting the value they feel they deserve for the hours they're working. They may even have trouble envisioning how they can move into a high-end way of pricing, by selling a transformation or by selling outcomes where there's certainly a lot more value. Being able to make the shift to asking for the value of a transformation is a big stretch.

Pricing the value based on how much that transformation is worth to someone's life, that's where it can be interesting when you really do the calculation.

Charging fees such as $250 or $350 an hour can be a real challenge, because most of our population aren't used to paying those kinds of rates. They see it as a big amount of dollars to pay per hour. What's really interesting is when you look instead at the value that you give. When you tell them they are paying for the result that they really want and that it is going to cost them $5,000, if they want it badly enough, they'll buy it.

In actual fact, it might only be taking 5 or 10 hours of your time but now they aren't counting. In all our years in this business, we've only had two people who actually went back and divided the hours into the program price to figure what they were paying hourly. At $5,000, for 10 hours of work over the next 60 days, we'd be looking at $500 hourly. If we had tried using the fee for service approach to get someone at even half that, at $250 an hour, it would have a much harder task. Start pricing your products and services for the transformation they bring your ideal client.

Know How to Sell Your Outcome or Transformation

That's why it's so important to sell outcome or transformation. But it doesn't just benefit you. Selling and charging for a specific transformation also benefits your clients. If someone hires a coach for $300 an hour, they are looking for ways to cut down the number of hours they use. But when they pay $5,000 for an outcome, they are doing everything they can to get the most out of the time they have with you. They come with all their homework done and you literally just have to tweak things to get them the transformation they want. They do it all themselves because you had the balls to charge them a high price.

Know How to Value and Price Yourself

The price that you can ask for your products and services is in direct relation to the value that you feel you can support. In most cases, when someone has difficulty charging a high fee, they have a hard time with their personal value. This is a very important area of personal growth. Developing your worthiness is the fastest way to move out of the fee for service model and into the high fee for transformation model.

We can often see the value that people bring to their clients much more clearly than they can. They are often too close to it and too wrapped up in it. We look at how bad their client's life would be without the service and put a price figure on the cost of the loss. These numbers can get very large. After that, it is up to the person offering the service to have a personal value that supports charging that fee.

Charge What You're Worth

When you look at the benefit that your client is getting from having hired you, look at how their life is changing. Consider all the things that they are now capable of doing in their lives because of their interaction with you.

Dr. Paul When I was in private practice, many of my patients would quit jobs, start or end relationships and make huge life changes that were supportive of who they really were. I would coach them in ways that helped them to break through barriers and beliefs they had about themselves so they could be happier and healthier. But, as a chiropractor, I was only getting paid the same amount per

visit as the guy down the street who could have someone in and out in three minutes.

In Canada, the industry standard for an adjust-
ment is $50. If I wanted to charge what I'm worth,
I'd need to quadruple my rates. No one will pay that.
But if I take my transformation to another industry,
like the personal development industry where there is
no price point, I can charge whatever I want. In the
personal growth and development industry, people will
pay anything from next to nothing to $100,000 for a
transformation if you can ask for it.

If you're confined by industry standards, search for more
inventive and interesting ways to look at charging your value.
Maybe even cross into another industry. When you get good
at charging what you're worth, and if you follow the principles
that we've been teaching in this book, then you can start living
really well.

How Do You Engage Your Clients Long Term?

Package Your Services So Clients are Enrolled Long Term

There's no better way to get off the whole commodity track
than positioning yourself as a Celebrity Expert with a book.
It's also a great way to engage your clients long term. In general, a client who comes to you through your book will stay
with you three times longer, will spend three times as much

money, and will refer you ten times as often.

Your book, when written properly, shows them that there's a bigger picture to what you do. They can see that their time with you, or the interaction that they have with you, fulfilled their need, but there's still more they can learn from you. And that's also what you want to do with your products and services. Always show them what the next step is. "We are complete with what we agreed to do, and this is where you're at, and this is the next place that you could go." If you always have that philosophy and you always have the next program or the next package, then you can keep a client with you longer. It's so much easier to keep them long term than to keep searching for new clients. It's better for the long-term client and it's better for you.

Have Programs and Packages to Upsell

Having more value that you can offer a client than they have already agreed to receive is a great way to keep clients longer or sell more to them. An upsell is something you can offer your clients while they are already receiving one level of service from you, but you think a higher level will provide them with a bigger and better level of the transformation they desire. If you have something that offers them even more value that they can add on, then it's a way to make another sale and to add more value to their lives. It's not just a matter of always trying to sell people more. It's win-win because the customer is more satisfied and you make more money serving a happy client. When you're doing it in integrity, upselling becomes a very natural thing that they are very grateful for.

Chunk Your Content into Manageable Parts

Chunking your content into manageable parts is an important part of creating your specialized system, but it also serves you by improving your profitability. Because each chunk is easier to complete and understand, clients are more satisfied with the outcome. On top of it, you have the next chunk to offer them when they are done.

One of the biggest mistakes that people make is they think that over-delivering content equals over-delivering value. This just overwhelms and confuses a client, which leads to frustration and a decreased perception of value. Make sure that you can pick one thing that you're going to change or transform for that client, and do it really well. They will appreciate that so much more than getting a whole lot of different things to work on and nothing gets completed. If what you have in your program looks over-optimistic for the timeframe, don't try to fit all those pieces into that package. You'll shine brighter if you go for a ten out of ten on a smaller section rather than going for a six out of ten on multiple sections.

Deliver Exceptional Value on One Specific Part of Your Content

Delivering exceptional value on a very specific part of your content is the ultimate in specialization. You can customize your system to the client's needs if you have a series of high-end pieces you can put together. You'll not only sell it for more money but there is always a next step for the client.

What Group Programs Do You Offer to Leverage Your Time?

Leveraging yourself and operating group programs can expand your business, as well as give good value to your clients.

Hold Workshops to Deliver Your Content to Groups

Sometimes you'll find that there are steps in your process that you repeat with every single client. This takes up time that you could be using to deliver specialized value to your clients. If you can get a group of clients together and deliver the same content so they're all grasping it at the same time, that leverages, or actually duplicates, you. Now you're serving many people at the same time instead of one at a time.

When you have a practice full of people and you're serving one person at a time, it gets to the point where you want to clone yourself. A leveraged group program allows that delivery of transformation with less effort on your part.

You start charging different rates for different levels of access. Clients will definitely value one-on-one time when you have your eyes on them exclusively, and this can be charged at a premium. It does become more expensive to work with you privately but because the repetitive material is offered in a lower priced group program, when clients have specialized time with you, you can do your best work with them. The group program will have brought them to a point further along in your system and you will help them one-on-one with the parts they can't do on their own.

You can also leverage parts of your program by actually recording programs and then create audio-based packages they

can do on their own and products that they can purchase.
Then, you're looking at the wonders of creating income with
work that has already been done.

Teach Courses and Programs on Your Content

Having a best-selling book, and positioning yourself as
a Celebrity Expert Author, is a very powerful form of leverage. Combining this with doing a workshop that delivers your
own content really positions you to a further height. Having
your own course adds to that credibility and your celebrity. It
gives people somewhere to go from your book and it leverages the information because the book may even be a textbook
or a guide for the course. By taking your information and
repurposing it, you're getting more value and more streams of
income from the same content.

The courses and programs that operate on your content
don't have to be anything different from what's in your book.
The delivery style is different, and the way they take in and use
the information will have a different outcome. A lot of times
you can do these workshops and then take that workshop and
video it, or livestream it, so people who aren't even present can
benefit from the course.

Develop Group Training Programs

Group training programs are a great way to free up your
time and increase your income when you have filled up your
hours with one-on-one clients. If you are just starting out, it
can be more difficult to start with group training. It is often
better to walk a few clients through your material one-on-one
to get a feel for its delivery. Once your time is beginning to

be a limiting factor, then develop the group training program. When there is demand for your service, your clients won't question why they don't have your undivided attention. It they want that, they will have to pay extra.

Teach Online Training Programs

The amazing thing about this industry is that you don't end up having to work in any geographic location to reach your clients. If you can plug in and connect, you can reach people. If you've taken your content and you've built it into training programs, then you can get people together, no matter where they are in the world, by bringing them into a virtual classroom and delivering your content. You can even charge the same prices as if you were doing it in person.

How Does Your Product Suite Showcase Your Services and Expertise?

Create Your Products in Digestible Chunks

Through the simplicity of chunking your material, and the elegance of packaging it into exceptional bits of value, you end up with a product suite. With time, and by working with the Elements we have described in this book, your content just starts to build up until you have a number of entry points for clients to engage with you. Your book will always have the element of an upsell in it, because, with the Celebrity Expert Author book, the whole point is that it's going to promote your product suite.

It can start as simply as a pre-recorded course that is on your website, that people buy for $297. This would have a natural upsell to something that would involve more of your time and energy, like a group course, where they will receive more guidance from you. You can have a whole suite of different options for them to work with you. For example, someone who wants to learn to be a Celebrity Expert Author would want to use a product suite that contained products that helped them clarify their transformation and position their service, write copy with powerful calls-to-action, create course content and deliver great talks. That's what a product suite is.

Always keep your programs and products in easily digestible chunks so you don't overwhelm your clients. Most of us err on the side of too much content, which is often detrimental to helping your clients. When people get confused or overwhelmed, they stop and never pay attention again. They don't come back to it and the content or the program becomes something to do or revisit at a later date. They don't progress and they don't get the outcome.

If you have things in digestible chunks that you know people can complete, they can benefit from the transformation quickly. When they see results, they want to continue to see new results.

If you have three big concepts in one package, and each concept has a lot of work involved in it, consider breaking it down into three packages. That way your clients can gain completion on each package before progressing to the next one. Everyone will do better this way.

Fit Your Products Together in a Progression

When your product suite is grouped this way, a natural

progression to what you have to offer unfolds. When you look at or use your older packages, you often begin to see where things are clumped together. For example, perhaps there is some specific material that you want to give to a particular client but it's buried in the middle of a big program. The rest of the program becomes a distraction to the focus and outcome you currently want for the client. It might not even be time for them to receive those additional pieces of your transformation.

By having separate products that can fit together in a progression, you have the flexibility to work with clients who are at different stages or who come in from different avenues.

Move and Upsell Your Clients Through Your Product Suite

This really speaks to the earlier Critical Element 2, where we were talking about making your services marketable to the ideal client, and wanting to narrow your services and keep them relevant to the transformation. If all your products and services are key parts of delivering the transformation, including that one special over-arching transformation that you deliver to your target audience, they will see that they need all those parts. The upsell is almost a natural progression. If it's logical and it's built right in, you actually don't really have to do anything to get them to continue.

Launch Your Products

A launch simply means having a sale, or getting everybody interested in doing something at the same time. It doesn't have to be anything fancy like a big internet launch that takes all sorts of time and effort to prepare. It's simply a matter of creating a stir, or an interest in your product or service, so you can generate a bunch of sales all at the same time.

Having a product launch can be as simple as doing a mailing to your list and saying, "We're having a special". Or you can get on the phone to people who've already bought from you, tell them about a new program you just put together, and get them all to enroll. It might be hosting an event and getting people to come to it. There's so many ways that you can do a launch, but most people make it too complicated. Because their methods for launching are so complex, all their energy goes into building the launch platform and nothing goes into generating revenue. One of the simplest ways to get people engaged is to talk to them.

An important key to success is to set a goal or a target for your launch, and adapt when you see that one product you've developed is not hitting your numbers. Even if the first launch doesn't achieve your target, it doesn't mean that you can't achieve that goal in the longer run if you adjust your approach.

Bob We recently did a webinar for a book project and we had 350 people at the webinar. The goal was to get 10% of them involved in the project. Of the 350 people, 3 people converted into the book project. That didn't mean that we failed: it just meant that the webinar wasn't the venue or the way to reach that goal. The person who taught was a master at doing webinars, but in this particular application, it just didn't work. We ended up sending out personal emails to this person's list. The email took them to an application process, which was followed up by a personal phone call where we showed them how this could really benefit them and their business. We went from 3 conversions to 41 conversions.

Always have a goal, because it keeps you focused on where you're going. If you don't have a focus, you won't get there. It's as simple as that. Put your goal down on paper and look at it every day. By keeping your focus on what you want to achieve, you'll not only start coming up with all sorts of ideas, but you'll also see the synchronicities and chance encounters that will get you there.

One of our favorite philosophies is that "Old school is the new school". When the trendy marketing approaches stop working, you can always go back to the tried and true methods of personal contact with people. Everyone is trying the latest method of creating connection and rapport through impersonal means, but it all comes down to the fact that people like people.

In the launch Bob was just talking about, the original list was 200,000; 2,200 signed up for the webinar; 350 came to the webinar; and 3 converted. Everybody falls in love with that the idea of organizing a push-button webinar over the internet. And, for some, it can still be a successful launch, but as a methodology, it was a lot more powerful 5 or 10 years ago. The one approach that always works, and always will work, is getting out there, positioning yourself with your book and doing speeches. Old school is the new school. In fact, the results tend to get better every year as people become more disillusioned with the lack of human connection. And that's the application of what we're talking about in this very book.

—⚬—

With this 5th Critical Element under your belt, you now know where the real money lies as an author. Mastering this content will make you step into your role as the specialist and get you away from charging dollars for hours. Packaging your materials and making sure they are delivered in digestible chunks will help you keep your clients engaged long term and wanting a steady stream of your valuable solutions.

As your celebrity grows and you start to find that your time is becoming the limiting factor in how you serve clients, you will want to seek ways to leverage yourself. When the enviable problem of having too many clients hits, you will want to consider group programs and products that deliver value to your clients without taking so much of your time.

Your specialized programs will evolve as you do and the way that you serve your target audience must always continue to improve. Stay abreast of these 5 Critical Elements and review and add to your worksheets on a regular basis. This 5th Element is the place where you can truly design your 7-Figure Business.

Conclusion

*T*here are so many marketing trends out there that it is hard to know what will work for you in your business. With new gimmicks and conversion techniques popping up all the time, it is easy to get distracted and caught up in chasing the latest method that promises to give you the big payoff. That is why we have kept our focus on the tried and true methods that will never lose their appeal.

Old school is the new school as far as we're concerned. People will always respond to books in print, a well delivered speech and the personal connection. These old school approaches will always reach people and are the foundation of the 5 Critical Elements of the Celebrity Expert Author. Become proficient in the following 5 Critical Elements and you will guarantee yourself success:

1. Identify a target audience that you want to serve

2. Make your services marketable to the target audience you've chosen to serve

3. Write the book that makes your target audience hungry for your services

4. Speak and network within your target audience in the places they congregate

5. Offer your specialized programs to your target audience on the back-end

If you apply even 10% of what we have shared here, you will dramatically reduce the level of struggle in your business. You'll be one of the 0.1% in the expert industry who enjoy a steady stream of ideal clients and a 6 to 7 figure income. Use your results from the self-assessment at www.CelebrityExpertAuthorQuiz.com as a benchmark as you work through the worksheets for each Element. You will notice that the contents of this book have already coached you into the right mindset for success in this industry.

Now you need to build the components of your Celebrity Expert Author Signature System. They come directly from the 5 Critical Elements and our own business model is built from them.

Components of the Celebrity Expert Author Signature System include:

1. A Rock Solid Promise that tells ideal clients the transformation they can expect

2. A High-End System for delivering the results of your transformation

3. The Right Book that positions you as the expert to your ideal clients

4. A Compelling Talk that converts

5. A Quiz that positions your leads for your high-end programs